IMAGES OF WALES

NEWPORT PEM.
AND FISHGUARD
REVISITED

IMAGES OF WALES

NEWPORT PEM. AND FISHGUARD REVISITED

MARTIN LEWIS

TEMPUS

Frontispiece: Caersalem Chapel Choir, 1904/5 comprised of, from left to right, back row: Benjamin Howells, Cilgwyn; David Eynon Griffiths, Trewern; James Bowen, Ty'r Iet; James Howell Rees, Sychpant; Revd J.L.I. Morris (Minister); Thomas Thomas, Gwaunydd (Conductor); Richard Howells, Drefach; Johnny Griffiths, Trewern. Middle row: Amelia Bowen, Ty'r Iet; Sarah James, Pant y Graig; Dorothy Ann Williams, Argoed; Elizabeth M. Griffiths, Trewern; Ann Bowen, Ty'r Iet; Mary Ann Griffiths, Trewern; Mary Ann Howells, Cilgwyn. Front row: Mary and David Bowen, Ty'r Iet; and Mary Jane and David Gwion Howells of Cilgwyn.

First published 2003

Tempus Publishing Limited
The Mill, Brimscombe Port,
Stroud, Gloucestershire, GL5 2QG

© Martin Lewis, 2003

The right of Martin Lewis to be identified as the Author of this work has been asserted in accordance with the Copyrights, Designs and Patents Act 1988.

British Library Cataloguing in Publication Data.
A catalogue record for this book is available from the British Library.

ISBN 0 7524 3040 8

Typesetting and origination by Tempus Publishing Limited
Printed in Great Britain by Midway Colour Print, Wiltshire

Contents

Foreword

In this fascinating sequel to his first volume, Martin Lewis has, once again, struck a rich vein of material relating to the social history of North Pembrokeshire during the last hundred years or so – a selection of photographic and other material which provides a penetrating insight into the social habits, customs and idiosyncrasies of the population of the area since the early 1900s. Images in his first volume were substantially drawn from his vast collection of postcards of the area. By contrast, in this volume, he has made extensive use of photographs, documentation, anecdotal evidence and historical narrative, and the volume is the richer for it. The very nature of the book demands that the author should paint his picture on a broad canvas, and this he has done in a very effective manner, and with an intimacy which only a resident of the area could do.

He presents his material with both humour and sadness and in some places it is presented without comment, leaving the reader to make up his own mind. He reminds us of the momentous changes which affected each and every one of us during the twentieth century, from the days of large families, the influence of the church and chapels on the social scene, the march of education, the improvement in communication systems, the advancement of technology, and changes in our modes of transport, the change from the sail of small coastal schooners to the turbine-powered greyhounds of the Atlantic; the Ocean Expresses which travelled non stop from Paddington to Fishguard in under five hours; horse-drawn transport giving way to motorised cars and commercial vehicles, and finally, the promotion of aviation and local reaction of the public to it.

The collection in its entirety, particularly when read and viewed in conjunction with his first selection, provides a view on so many aspects of community life in the recent past. His photographic evidence places on record the way things were, and that in itself is very valuable. I have been absorbed and entertained by this second volume of his work, and am certain that it will bring to his readers the same enjoyment that it has given me.

It is my pleasure to commend the book to you.

Dr Geraint Jenkins

Dr Geraint Jenkins,
Curator (retired) Welsh Folk Museum (St Fagan's, Cardiff)
Curator (retired) Welsh Industrial & Maritime Museum
Lord High Sherriff of Dyfed 1994/95.
Chairman, Ceredigion County Council 2002/03.

The church tea party. Its organisers nearly always took participants to the seaside. The favoured few will have been carried to the beach by pony and trap, which might also have carried the food and utensils, but the great majority will have walked a few miles to get there. The photograph shows such a visit by church members of Llanllawer, to the beach at Pwllgwaelod in the early part of the century. Note the cast iron kettle and galvanised water cans.

Cotham Lodge at Newport was built by James Bevan Bowen of Llwyngwair as a dower house. It was built in 1789, and occupied by his widow following James' death in 1816. The widow had lived in a mansion at Cotham near Bristol, and hence the name of the lodge at Newport. It remained in the family for many years, but was sold following the First World War.

Introduction

Most counties throughout the country seem to produce their own amateur historians. In the twelfth century, Pembrokeshire had Giraldus Cambrensis. More specifically, Newport Pem. has produced a succession of such enthusiasts, the first of whom was the Elizabethan historian, George Owen of Henllys, Lord of Cemais in 1592, who wrote (using scribes) at least seventy learned papers, the earliest being written in around 1603. At the end of the nineteenth century, the Revd Evan Jones, incumbent at Newport, wrote his delightful book *A Historical Sketch of Newport, Pembrokeshire* (published 1890), and this without the assistance of photography. The late Mr Islwyn Jenkins, headmaster of the local primary school, took a keen interest in local history, having articles published in newspapers and editing the publication *Looking Around Newport* (1970). Dillwyn Miles has worn the mantle of Historian of Newport for the last half century, and incessantly and tirelessly researches and publishes the history of the district. Born and bred in Newport Pem., he is a veritable mine of information about the area, and has generously allowed me to draw on his work. I am deeply indebted to him for assisting me on so many occasions.

Like its predecessor, this book is intended to give a few glimpses of the social history of the community; in particular over the last one hundred years or so. This has been illustrated with postcards or photographs, wherever suitable material has emerged.

Many people have asked me how I have been able to amass such a collection of pictures and postcards, and many are under the impression that I have acquired these locally. This however is not true. Those people who spent their vacations at Newport in the first decades of the last century almost invariably sent their postcards away from the area. During the first ten years of the last century – the reign of King Edward VII – postcard collecting was almost a 'mania'. The postcards, like stamps, were kept in albums. Many of these albums have now found their way into dealer networks, and thus the postcards have become available for purchase. I have purchased most of my cards from places as far afield as Cardiff, Cheltenham, London, Twickenham, Birmingham, Nottingham, Yeovil and York.

There were several interesting reactions to my first book. A lady of limited means approached the local newsagent, stating that she wished to, but could not afford to buy the book. It was thus agreed that she should pay a £2 deposit followed by eight weekly instalments of £1. Another lady advised me that each morning at 11.00 o'clock, she had a cup of coffee, and looked at three of 'my pictures', always seeing something she had not spotted previously. It is also known that copies of the book have been stolen from at least three local hostelries, and it is gratifying at least to appreciate that the book was worth stealing! The author hopes that this volume will have just as much appeal, and bring the same enjoyment as did the first.

Martin Lewis

one

Approaches to Newport

The Pentre Ifan cromlech is undoubtedly the most famous of the cromlechs in the vicinity of Newport. It is some five miles out of the town (Map Ref. 139/100370). George Owen of Henllys made the first-known drawing of a cromlech which shows that Pentre Ifan has changed little since 1590. He described it as the most impressive stone structure he had ever seen, with the exception of Stonehenge in Wiltshire. A notice on the approach path stated that 'This monument was erected in the Neolithic Age (2,500 BC-1,000 BC) for the communal burial of the dead. It was probably covered with a mound of earth or stones and this has been partially restored'.

Two other cromlechs have survived in the area: Carreg Goetan Arthur 138/060393 (left, in the town of Newport) and Llech y Drybedd (139/100432) (right), near Moylegrove. The name, translated, means 'Tripod Stone.' It would have required a considerable human effort and feat of engineering to place a capstone, weighing many tons, on its supports.

The fort at Castell Henllys (145/116390). This site is run by the Pembrokeshire Coast National Park and is the only 'on site' reconstruction of an Iron Age fort (from around 400 BC) in Britain. Excavations have established that there were a number of round houses and rectangular buildings here – probably used for storing grain or domestic animals – and that the facilities could have supported a community of up to one hundred people. Smelting of iron ore was undertaken, the iron being used for tools and weapons.

Gentry houses near Newport. Penbenglog overlooks the Duad Valley, and was the home of the antiquary and a patron of the bards, George William Griffith (1580-1655). It was also the birthplace of Sir Watkin Lewes MP, the only Pembrokeshire born Lord Mayor of London. He was born in 1740 and was part of the Griffith family.

Public transport at Eglwyswrw, *c.* 1922. Approximately six miles north of Newport Pem. stands the village of Eglwyswrw. The omnibus at the top of the hill is almost certainly the property of the Great Western Railway Company. The GWR was in fierce competition at that time with the service established by Howard Roberts of Newport. This enmity between bus companies extended throughout South Wales. The bus of one company would seek to anticipate the departure time of its competitor, and set off five minutes in advance with a view to collecting all passengers en route.

The Sergeants' Inn at Eglwyswrw (on the left), dates from medieval times, and occupies a prominent place in the village. It is said that 'peripatetic' barristers met here, and Fenton says of them that 'Here, during the stay of the itinerant counsel, a tribunal is constituted for trying all offences against the dignity of the bar, and amercing the delinquents; in carrying on which mock process, an infinite deal of wit, humour and festivity is excited... ' It is worth noting however that until relatively recently – around 1975 – the Eglwyswrw Magistrates met at this tavern.

The village church and school at Egwlyswrw – part of a scene which has since undergone complete change. The road at this point was widened in around 1997, and it was a very complex process to gain permission to remove 'consecrated ground' at this point. Some of the graves were estimated to date from the thirteenth century with some tombs being no greater than three feet in length. On the extreme left can be seen part of the original village school building.

The pupils of Eglwyswrw school in 1913, photographed in the grounds of the church. The age range of the boys and girls in this photograph (and the absence of a class number) suggests that this photograph shows all the pupils attending this school at that time (about forty). This school is now one of the most successful and flourishing schools in the area with a pupil population exceeding 130 (2002).

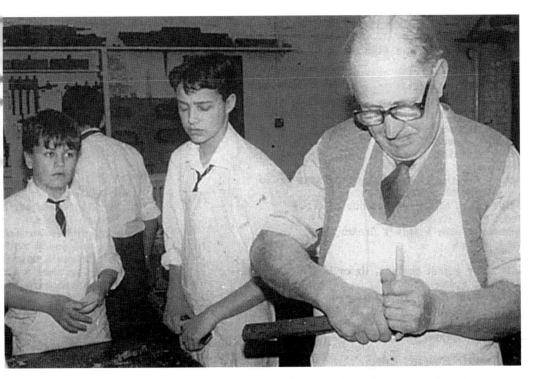

The Craftsman of Duad Valley, John Davies, or Jack y Bompren (Jack of the wooden bridge) as he was affectionately known, lived in close proximity to the Duad Brook, and worked on the railway which came down past his house. He was a skilled craftsman and carver of timbers, and took great delight in carving soup spoons and Welsh love spoons from the various timbers which grew all around him. He would talk with great enthusiasm, in particular to the patrons of the Salutation Inn in Felindre, where he sometimes assisted, about the ways in which the timber needed to be treated and stored prior to working it on his lathe and with hand tools. He often carved spoons to mark specific occasions. The above photograph shows him passing on some of the skills of his craft to a pair of youngsters from Ysgol y Preseli. He was a very devout man who worshipped at Meline church, which was a distance of some three field widths from his home, a weekly trek which he undertook without fail. He would gladly conduct a church service when called upon to do so. On one occasion his friend, the Most Revd George Noakes was being consecrated as Archbishop of Wales at Bangor (North Wales) and Jack was unable to go. As an alternative, he acquired a copy of the consecration service for Archbishops, went alone to Meline church, and worked his way through the entire service at the very time that his friend was being consecrated.

Opposite above: Crymmych Arms station, *c.* 1935. This was the destination for lorries arriving with loads of timber from the Duad Valley. From here, it would be transported to the Welsh valleys where the timber would be used as pit props in the coal mines. The station was on the Whitland to Cardigan line, which was opened to passengers in 1875. It is said however that, even before this time, a person could travel as 1 cwt or 1½ cwts of freight depending on his/her dimensions!

Opposite below: A small narrow guage railway line was built to carry wood from the top of the Pengelly forest to a point at the bottom, half a mile from the confluence of the Duad with the River Nevern. Here is an example of one of the steam lorries employed to carry timber from this point to the Great Western station at Crymych, for distribution to the Welsh valleys.

The common at Brynberian, *c.* 1926. The main road from the bridge on the left is that from Cardigan to Haverfordwest (B4329). At this point, it passes a piece of common land adjacent to the village of Brynberian. Sheep are allowed to graze the Preseli Hills in the background. Once a year, they are gathered in their thousands at this point in an event known as 'Y Stra', and identified by ear marks prior to selling. Sheep not so identified are sold separately, and proceeds divided among the local villagers holding common rights. The parked vehicles in the picture reflect the numbers of people attending the Gymanfa Fawr in 1926.

Llwynihirion council school, *c.* 1917. Sometimes known as the Board school, Cross Roads it was opened in 1878 with the capacity to take eighty children. The average attendance however was about forty-five, as shown above. The first headmaster was G.T. Miles. Many of the children were required to walk several miles to and from school each day in all weathers – winter and summer. It was also used as a social centre and electoral polling station as and when circumstances demanded. Sadly, the school was closed in 1972, purchased by the local people and is now used as a community centre.

The chapel played an important part in the life of the community in any village. Not only did it provide spiritual solace, fellowship, and the opportunity for communal worship; it also acted as a social centre. Baptismal, marriage and funeral services would be conducted here. Other social functions would include concerts, Eisteddfodau, parties and, of course, Sunday school outings for the children.

One of the most important dates in the chapel calendar however was Whit Monday when the Cymanfa Bwnc would be held in the chapel. This event stemmed from the time when the majority of people could not read. Over several preceding Sundays, the congregation would be required to learn a substantial portion of the scriptures, usually from the New Testament. The event is best described by Dillwyn Miles in his Portrait of Pembrokeshire. 'The whole gathering would chant the opening verses, then the young girls would stridulate the next few, the growing lads, with voices breaking, would skedaddle discordantly through theirs: then, in turn the middle aged female and male, the croaking old ladies, and finally, the old men with a thunderous boom, before the masses came in again with the closing verses.'

Opposite above: Capel Bach, Brynberian, *c.* 1905 The construction of the chapel commenced in 1690 and it was here that the Congregational Movement began in North Pembrokeshire. From 1743 to 1764, the Minister was one Revd David Lloyd. His brother Thomas had charge of Bethel chapel in Moylegrove until 1770. Under the auspices of Brynberian chapel, services were regularly conducted in the town of Newport from the early part of the eighteenth century onwards (see p.46)

The village of Felindre Farchog. This postcard bears a postmark from 1921. At the near left can be seen the roof of the 'college' established by George Owen of Henllys for the education of his children. At the bottom right was a small enclosure (not visible in the picture) which was used as an animal pound. Stray animals would be kept here until claimed (against a fee) by their owners. It often happened that the fee payable exceeded the value of the animal. The road through the village is now the main A487 and the first building on the right was the original chapel at Felindre.

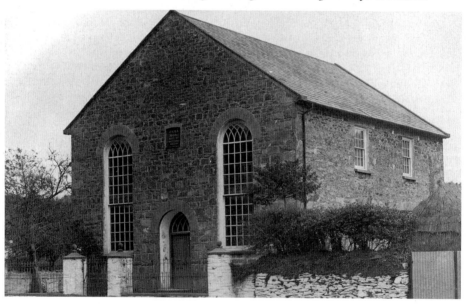

The chapel at Felindre. Although there may have been another building before this, the original chapel was built at Felindre in 1810. Services were run under the auspices of the movement at Brynberian. With the fear of punishment removed (for non-conformist worship), and the rapidly swelling congregations, the building soon became inadequate, and in 1857, Cana chapel (above) was opened. To the right of these premises was Y Felin, the mill where farmers took their grain to be ground. It is also thought that, at one time, there was a tannery in the village.

One of the bridges at Felindre. It is not known exactly when this arched and stone structure was built, or indeed whether it was the original bridge. The photograph dates from 1908.

Felindre was a staging post for the mail coach from Cardigan to Fishguard, and there would be a change of horses at the Salutation Inn in the village. The bridge was sufficient, of course, for carrying a single vehicle at a time (as indeed the bridge at Nevern is now). However, with the increase in traffic of the 1920s it became woefully inadequate, and was eventually replaced by this bridge in 1923, built by Fothergill's of Exeter.

St Brynach's church, Nevern, 1913. This church was founded by St Brynach in the sixth century, and this makes it one of the oldest churches in North Pembrokeshire. It is late Perpendicular in style and cruciform in plan. The tower however is Norman and houses a total of six bells which were cast by Thomas Rudhall of Gloucester in 1763. Each bell bears a different inscription indicating the names of the donors. They have a total weight of $1\frac{1}{2}$ tons. One bell marks the Golden Jubilee of Queen Victoria in 1887.

St Brynach's church hall. Built as a memorial hall in 1908, it is situated across the road from the entrance gate to the churchyard. It is frequently used for church functions, art exhibitions, committee and other meetings. This forms a background for the two young ladies enjoying an afternoon drive in their new Morris 12, one of whom is Mrs Vera Morgan. Her father, Mr Tom Evans ran a drapery and gents' outfitter's store at Manchester House in Market Street, Newport.

The chapel at Nevern. David Griffiths was appointed tutor to the children of the Bowen family at Llwyngwair in 1774. Following ordination, he arranged for the chapel (centre left) to be built for use by the Bowen family. This was used for week-day meetings by the Methodists. However, with the parting of the ways between the Methodists and the Church in Wales in 1811, the building became redundant. Following the Education Act of 1870, a Board school was established on this site. This served the community until its closure in 1961, and the building is now a village hall.

Llwyngwair Lodge stands on the main A487 road. This card is postmarked 1913. The lodge stands at the entrances to the grounds of the house at Llwyngwair, and with windows at regular intervals in the circular exterior of the building, the gatekeeper could see all comings and goings to and from the house. The main route to Llwyngwair since 1891 has been along the sweeping drive shown here, and across an open meadow. The former drive – now the tradesman's entrance, is to the left of the lodge.

The village at Nevern comprises of little more than can be seen in this image. It was however a complete community with its own church, school, village hall, post office and tavern. The Caman Brook – no more than ten feet wide and crossed by a pedestrian bridge, flows between St Brynach's church and the vicarage (out of shot on the right-hand side) In the late 1990s a flash flood swelled the river to such an extent that it lifted a stone bridge, causing it to collapse into the river, uprooted trees, and even carried cars downstream.

Mr William Rodgers died on 4 June 1806. It must be assumed that he was a son of Nevern, because his mother, brother and sister all lived in close proximity to the community. He must have been a remarkable man for, at some stage in his life, he left Nevern and went to make his fortune in London. It would have taken a great deal of courage for, at the end of the eighteenth century, little was spoken in this district other than the Welsh language, and the ability to speak the English language in the vicinity was exceptional. Linguistic difficulties coupled with the shock of the cultural change must have made life difficult for him. We can only infer from his will that he was a married man without children, and that he became a wealthy merchant living in the Kensington area of London. During his lifetime, he purchased the estate at Penrallt, Nevern. In his will, he left the house to his mother during her lifetime, and various parts of the estate to his brother, James, and his sister Margaret, during their lives, and thereafter to their two sons. He left the sum of £40 to his housekeeper, Mary Satter, twenty guineas to his cousin Sarah Edwards, housekeeper to the Duke of Marlborough and sums of £10 and mourning rings to various others as tokens of his esteem and affection.

He also held certain stocks including £800 invested in 3% consols, and he 'desired that the same [interest and dividends] be laid out annually in the manner following: 'one Moiety [part] thereof in good beef and the other Moiety thereof in good barley, and the same be distributed on every St Thomas' Day [21 December] in every year by the Minister and Church Wardens of the said Parish [Nevern].'

In 1895, the proceeds were used to purchase 505 lbs of beef (at 6d per lb)and fifty bushels of barley at 3s 4d per bushel. 124 people came forward to receive the benefit. The practice was discontinued during the Second World War years. Following this however, the accumulated dividends were sufficient to buy six quarters of beef (One and a half beasts!). This was supplied by Tommy Davies (butcher) of Pontycwm, and thereafter continued by his son Glyndwr, and in recent years by his son Iwan Davies. Ten people came forward in 2002 to receive beef valued at £32, half of which had been donated by local butcher, Paul James.

Nevern Bridge, *c.* 1910. Many local people contend that the 'handouts' emanating from the will of William Rogers should a) be made available only to the less well-off in the community, and b) that the practice should continue for so long as water flowed under Nevern Bridge. There is nothing in the will however to confirm that this was the intention of the deceased.

This view of the River Nevern is taken from the bridge looking upstream in or around 1905. The horse and cart (middle distance) is pulling out from the Trewern Arms – a centuries old 'hostelrye' where many business transactions took place between dealers and local farmers. The River Nevern has been renowned for many years for the sewin (migratory trout) and salmon fishing which it provides.

Nevern school, 1914. A senior class poses for a photograph in the presence of Miss Hannah Davies and the headmaster Alfred Ward. He was a strict disciplinarian and had no knowledge of the Welsh language. All lessons were taught in English, and this must have been an ordeal for children who spoke nothing but Welsh at home. The last child caught speaking Welsh on any given day would be caned the following day. Alfred Ward was headmaster for forty-one years.

Nevern school, c. 1923. W.J. Edwards, a Welsh speaking native of Glamorgan was the headmaster for the ensuing thirty-six years. By contrast, he was a very gentle and lenient man. Here, forty-two children pose for the photograph outside one of the school windows. At the outbreak of the Second World War, the school population almost doubled when about forty-five children aged between three and twelve were evacuated to the district from London – a sudden influx which most rural schools would welcome nowadays!

ELECTION

OF

RURAL DISTRICT COUNCILLORS

FOR THE

RURAL DISTRICT OF SAINT DOGMELLS,

IN THE YEAR 1894.

MORFA WARD

OF THE PARISH OF NEVERN.

NOTICE IS HEREBY GIVEN,

1. That a Poll for the Election of Rural District Councillors for the above-named Ward will be held on TUESDAY, the 18th day of December, 1894, between the hours of Four and Eight in the Afternoon.

2. That the number of Rural District Councillors to be elected for the Ward is One.

3. That the names in alphabetical order, places of abode, and descriptions of the Candidates for election, and the names of their respective Proposers and Seconders, are as follows :—

Names of Candidate (Surname first).	Place of Abode.	Description.	Names of Proposer (Surname first).	Names of Seconder (Surname first).
Evans, John	Glasdir	Farmer	Williams, William	Evans, Rees
Lamb, Thomas	Tredrissi-fach	Minister of the Gospel	James, William	James, Thomas
Lewis, Evan	Blaenmeini	Farmer	Marsden, James	Rowe, John

4. The situation of the Polling Place and Polling Station is as follows :—

THE BOARD SCHOOL AT NEVERN (WEST END).

5. The Poll will be taken by Ballot, and the colour of the ordinary Ballot Paper used in the Election will be White.

Dated this 10th day of December, 1894.

DAVID DAVIES,

25, Quay Street, Cardigan.

RETURNING OFFICER.

J. C. ROBERTS, PRINTER, "OBSERVER" OFFICE, 1, EBEN'S-LANE, CARDIGAN.

An election poster for Morfa Ward from 1894. The Morfa Ward of Nevern shares boundaries with those of Newport and Moylegrove, and is bounded by the River Nevern and Cardigan Bay to the south and west, and Moylegrove to the north. Nearly all constituents are of farming stock.

Gentry houses near Newport, Llwyngwair, *c.* 1950. There is evidence to indicate that the Cole family lived at Llwyngwair before 1326. They were farmers of some distinction who, like all farmers, wished to maximise productivity. George Owen contends that Cole was the first man in the district to use marl 'for the mending of the lands' and further that this marl (clay) was first discovered at Llwyngwair. It has a high calcium content, and thus has a beneficial effect on local acidic soils. The premises were acquired by the Bowens in 1503, and thirteen generations of the family lived there until 1955, each generation producing a male heir up to this time. The house was purchased by Sir James Bowen for his son Mathias, and it was he and his family who were its first Bowen occupants. The house later had six hearths, and a large number of bedrooms. They entertained extensively, particularly in connection with the Methodist faith. John Wesley and William Williams (Pantycelyn) were regular visitors to Llwyngwair, and following a Methodist Sasiwn in 1786, Williams records that 'Mr Bowen treated the whole association. Hundreds of people, godly and ungodly, dined and were entertained. Sixty beds were occupied by strangers at Llwyngwair alone, and about six score sat down to meals there.'

Opposite above: Gentry houses near Newport. Bury (or Berry) Hill House and Farm stands about half a mile north of the bridge at Newport. At one time, it was the property of the Barony of Cemais, and considered to be the granary of the castle at Newport. It was purchased by George Bowen of Llwyngwair in 1779, and occupied by members of the family for some time after. Soon after the end of the First World War, a substantial piece of land at the western extremity was sold for the purposes of creating the Newport golf course.

Opposite below: Threshing day at Berry Hill Farm, *c.* 1900. This was a very important day in the calendar of the farming community. The corn sheaves have been safely gathered (right). The threshing machine takes centre stage, and is belt driven by the traction engine on the left. This was always a communal effort when the farmers from the locality would all gather for this 'heavy' day. The maids have clearly just arrived with the tea. Nowadays of course, the whole job is managed by a couple of men and a combine harvester.

The bridge at Newport was built in 1894. George Owen of Henllys contends that the original bridge at Newport was a six-arched structure, constructed near the location of the present bridge. Early in the sixteenth century, a sweating sickness swept the country. It seems that it first hit Pembrokeshire at Milford in the year 1483, and it was claimed at the time that it afflicted only English people, for the Welsh and Scots living in the area were relatively unaffected. Shortly afterwards, the town of Newport was hit, and its effect on the townsfolk was devastating. So convinced were the people of Newport that the disease had spread to the town from the Morfa district, that it is said that they destroyed the bridge in their endeavours to control the spread of the disease. For some years, a ferry service was run by a lady about two hundred yards below the present bridge. She became known as Mali'r Cwch, (Mali of the boat) and when she died, the service was carried on by the mother and daughter Elizabeth and Hannah Davies.

Before the new bridge was built, Mr John Laugharne, a farm servant at Berry Hill, had been to Fishguard Harbour (Lower Town) to collect a consignment of goods. On his return journey, he stopped at the Golden Lion to quench his thirst. He tarried for a while, and when crossing the ford, the pair of horses and loaded wagon negotiated the incoming tide, but, when it arrived back at Berry Hill, there was no sign of the driver. During a search the following morning, his body was found in the estuary.

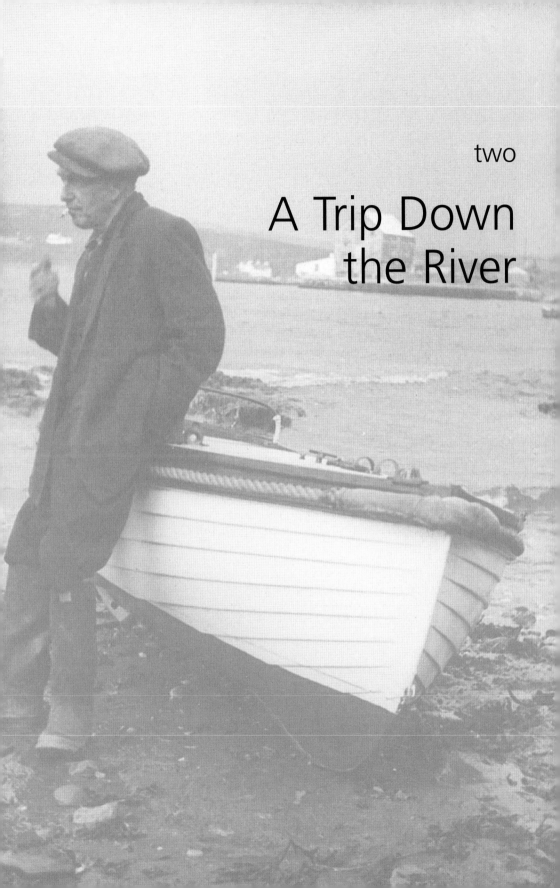

two

A Trip Down
the River

The stepping stones at Newport: were placed across the river when it was decided that the effects of the sweating sickness had subsided. This was an attempt to promote traffic once more. The disadvantage however was that the steps could only be used at low tide. The Ordnance Survey map for 1888 indicates there was a ford just below this point for horse-drawn traffic.

Newport shipyards. It was on this mud flat, some 400 yards below the bridge, that ship building in Newport took place. This was one of the largest ship-building sites in the whole of South Wales. Around sixty ships were built here between 1760 and 1860, some with a displacement of nearly 200 tons. Until relatively recently (about 1980), the remains of ships' hulls could be seen at this site at low tide, and it continued to be used as a maintenance and repair yard into the beginning of the last century. Most of these ships were built by John Havard and later by his son Levi.

The limekiln at Bryncyn was one of a number built near the water's edge on the River Nevern, and can just be seen, clad in ivy in the previous picture. Recently however, it has been refurbished to its original condition. Ships could only discharge at this particular kiln on the higher tides. The kiln would have been used to serve the farms on the Morfa.

The buildings at the Parrog. Mortuary No. 1. The eastern-most brook which flows through Newport is called Afon Ysgolheigion (Scholars' Brook), and it enters the estuary after crossing the marsh. Legend has it that about 500 years ago a building was erected near this point (below the bridge), and that it was used as a mortuary when the sweating sickness hit the town.

When it was taken over by E.D. Llewellyn early in the last century, it contained a number of thick, rectangular slate slabs measuring about six feet by three feet on which bodies might have been laid out. These slabs proved useful when the building was used as a slaughter house where Llewellyn, and later Tommy Davies (Pontycwm) and his son Glyndwr did the slaughtering for many of the butchers of the town. The building was used for this purpose until the early 1960s. The stream adjacent was useful for the discharge of blood and entrails, much of which was consumed by large flocks of herring gulls. It was said that 'the rats were bigger than cats, and the eels like anacondas.' The image shows all that remains of a once busy site.

MARKET STREET, NEWPORT, Pem.

.... *192*

M ....

BOUGHT OF

E. D. LLEWELLYN,

FAMILY AND GENERAL BUTCHER.

I am returning Registration Book No N.Y 187 as Car has been scrapped

Freeman

E.D. Llewell

Left: The fate of Ianto Llewellyn's car. Many Welshmen named Evan (as was E.D. Llewellyn) were called Ianto. He was a very sociable character who loved to entertain. After visiting the slaughter house one day, his Morris Cowley Coupé (which had a dickey seat) ran into one of the deep ditches which ran along one side of the bottom end of Long Street.

Below left: A bill head from E.D. Llewellyn, disconsolately advising the licensing powers that the log book was being returned as the car had been scrapped.

Opposite above: Chains, pulleys and a tripod were used in a vain attempt to rescue the car. Five gentlemen assisted with this task. Nearest the camera stands Tommy Lewis (carpenter, Llwyngwair estate) and then, Evan (Ianto) Williams of the Glenbrook garage (next door to the Golden Lion) operating the lifting gear.

Opposite below: 'Riverslea', on the estuary. When the tide is high, the veranda of this house is cantilevered out over the river. When the tide is low, the river forms a deep narrow channel at this point. It was here that Thomas John Selby Davies of Dolwerdd operated his Golfer's ferry every day, after he had completed the morning's milk round. One day, Davies was thumbing a lift from Cardigan to Newport when David Rees came along in his two-seater Bull-nose Morris, and stopped. 'Who are you?' he asked. 'I'm Thomas John Selby Davies from Cwm Pen Craig Uchaf came the reply. 'Oh, – there's too many of you!' said Rees, and drove on.

"RIVERSLEE" NEWPORT. NO. 66.

Parrog and the estuary, *c.* 1928. From this photograph, it can be seen that the Parrog at this time remained a small community separate from the town of Newport. It also shows the extent of the golf club at this time, comprising of not much more than Mr Nurse's hut. Nurse served as the professional at the golf club for many years. 'Riverslea' (see previous picture) is just out of shot on the left of this photograph. There are those who remember up to fifty ships being tethered, bow to stern, in the foreground at this point, as they sheltered over the winter months.

Buildings at Parrog, *c.* 1908. The storehouses were, at this time, five in number, the two largest of which can be seen here. Both were owned at one time by the farmer E.J. Griffiths of Trewern (see p.120). With the decline in coastal trade following the First World War, the storehouse on the left was demolished and the stones were used to build the Newport Memorial Hall which was formally opened in 1923.

The limekiln keeper's house was built adjacent to one of the kilns, next to the sea shore at the Parrog. It was the keeper's job to light and fire the kilns as and when required. This would follow the arrival, by sea, of a load of limestone. The kiln was charged with layers of kindling and dry bracken, followed by alternate layers of coal and limestone. The residue falling through to the base would be removed by farmers and spread on the land to counter the acidity of the north Pembrokeshire soils.

The buildings at the Parrog. The equipment store and mortuary No. 2 were used to store the breeches buoy equipment owned by the Newport Parrog Rocket Brigade, and to store any dead bodies which might have been landed by visiting/trading vessels. The equipment owned by the Rocket Brigade was kept on standby to assist any vessels in difficulty near the Newport coast. The mortuary was used on one occasion only; to store the body of a vagrant who died whilst sleeping at the base of the cooling limekiln.

NEWPORT PEM

The coastal trade at Newport was at one time very brisk. Ships would sail up and down the river on high tide, and, following negotiation of Newport's notorious bar – which was no mean feat – they thereafter waited for the tide to recede. Merchants and farmers would approach the ships with horses and carts. Thereafter, they had a four-hour period to unload the goods, before the next tide lifted the boat again. Newport at one time may have been visited by up to six ships per week.

Coastal trading at Newport. The tide is high, a ship has just arrived and the crew is being landed by one of the men from the ferry boats. A number of people are sitting on the wall, perhaps waiting for loved ones, or for news from afar. Mortuary No.2 is visible in the centre of the image, and the limekiln keeper's house is to the right. The road alongside was used to carry limestone to the top of the kiln. The text on this card indicates that as a port, Newport at this time came under the jurisdiction of Cardigan.

The coastal trade at Newport. That the young men living on the Parrog would become seamen was almost inevitable. Here, three young men wait to join ship as they pose against the harbour wall. They are Mr Tom Richards, who lived at Fern Cottage, Mount Terrace; Jack Davies (Dandre); and Mr Reggie Davies, whose nephew still lives on Parrog Road.

There were at least four people who made their living by ferrying passengers from the ships, or across the river to Traeth Mawr (the big beach). Seen here is Jack Price, also known as 'Jack No Change'. He kept his money in his bedroom, and paid it into the bank just once a year. By the end of October, he had amassed so much coin that it was necessary for him to take it up to Lloyd's Bank in Bridge Street in a wheelbarrow!

The Last Boat
Home from Newport, Pem.

Left: The Newport ferry gained some notoriety, and became the subject of comic pictures and postcards in the early 1900s. One such famous artist was Cynicus, who made similar comic cards for a number of different holiday resorts.

Opposite below: The estuary and Dinas Head can be seen in this view taken from storehouse No. 1 – the building that, at present, houses Newport Boat Club. In addition to the remnants of a limekiln, the corrugated iron hut in the foreground was erected soon after the war, and used for the general storage of boating paraphernalia – oars, rowlocks, sails, etc. Its existence was relatively short lived.

TRAETH MAWR, NEWPORT PEM.

Very early in the last century, some of the mariners at Newport placed a very heavy chain across the river bed. With the ebb and flow of the tides, there was a substantial build-up of silt on either side of the chain, which in turn, provided a shallow crossing place for pedestrians and horse-drawn traffic. The gentleman seen here with his horse and cart is crossing the river, probably to fetch either seaweed for his garden or sand for building purposes.

THE ESTUARY AND DINAS HEAD.

Ebenezer Sunday School 1898

Ebenezer Sunday school on an outing, 1898. The three local chapels and St Mary's church generally used to have an annual Sunday school outing to Traeth Mawr. The town band, pictured here, was jointly engaged by them for the day. Each Sunday school would assemble at the Town Cross and the band would then march them down to the bridge. The children were in high spirits, each carrying his or her own cup for tea. Then came a trek through Park y Shippil to the Warren, where the women folk boiled water for the tea 'yn y badell bres' (in the big brass bowl). When all the schools were assembled on the Warren, the band would play folk songs and various pieces of music. After tea, games were played, races were run and sweets thrown and scrambled for. Among the older young people, games called 'Twos and Threes' and 'March' were very popular. Everybody really enjoyed these simple pleasures.

Later, the band would return via Parrog playing folk-dance music from the top of the lime kiln at Parrog and there the young people would dance late into the evening.

This photograph shows the band, under the conductorship of the late Evan Thomas, Gwaunydd, enjoying a rest on the Warren with the Ebenezer Sunday school, reputed to number about 300. Unfortunately the picture has been damaged over the years, and so only a fraction of the large group can be shown.

Opposite above: Sunday school outing, *c.* 1900. A similar arrangement would exist with the chapels of the Gwaun Valley, such as Caersalem and Jabez. On these occasions, the band would march out along the Cilgwyn Road, and rendezvous with participants at Ty Rhos, approximately a mile from the town centre. The entire entourage would then march through the town, led by the band, to the beach at Parrog. Here, Caersalem Sunday school is seen with one of the storehouses in the background. (Note the band at the top right of the picture).

Opposite below: Filming *Law and Disorder* at the Parrog. The seafront was used as a set for this film in 1965. It tells the story of a man who explains his long absences to his family by stating that he was 'a sailor at sea', or ' a missionary in Africa', when in reality, he was serving time in prison for various crimes he had committed.

In the meantime, his son grew up to enter the legal profession, officiating at the very courts at which his father was supposed to appear. In this image of the filming, Sir Michael Redgrave is proudly speaking of the fish he has caught, with a crowd of Newport Women's Institute members acting as extras. 'Police Sergeant' Meredith Edwards keeps them all under control.

41

Newport Regatta, 1951: The regatta is held in August of each year, and most of the competitions are now held in the Cwm – an area which becomes a veritable hive of activity throughout the summer months. In the background can be seen the former lifeboat house, opened in 1883, and closed only twelve years later. The lifeboat had been launched on three occasions only during that time.

Pulling the Seine net, c. 1900. This was an occupation which fed several families for many years, involving a rowing boat which was taken out from the shore in a large semi-circle, all the time feeding out a net, weighted and floated at its and lower and upper edges. The net was then pulled in by a team of four or six men. Today, only one licence is issued at Newport Pem. and there are strict rules governing its usage.

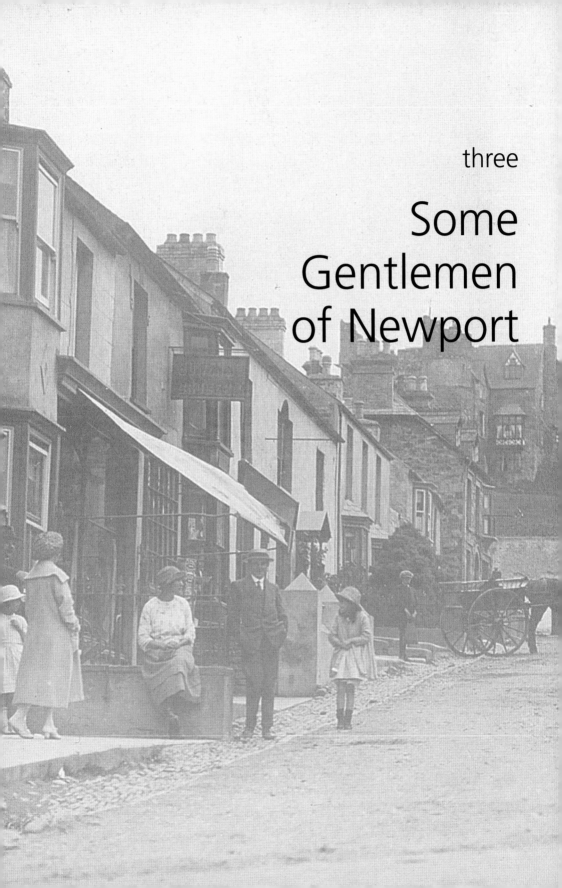

three

Some
Gentlemen
of Newport

Llys Meddyg is one of the larger houses in Newport Pem. This postcard bears the date 1921. When it was owned by Richard Jackson, it was the Prince of Wales public house, and it was from here that a daily coach was run to catch the train from Haverfordwest to London. Around 1865, the property was bought and rebuilt by Dr H. Bowen Perkins, (see p.56) and he named it Llys Meddyg – the Doctor's Court. The Golden Lion (formerly the Green Dragon), stands just beyond the house.

The entrepreneur of Newport Pem. It is not clear whether John George Isaac was born with a deformity to his legs or whether he contracted polio at an early age. He was however left with a severe handicap and a laboured walk. He built himself the flat cart above, and the small donkey pulled him wherever he wanted to go. From an early age, he provided a service to local farmers by trapping rabbits which he shipped in large quantities to the major conurbations, particularly during the Second World War. The outbreak of the disease myxomatosis in 1952 knocked the bottom out of his world, and, in effect, deprived him of his living. However, despite his disability, he was not one to sit back and retire into idleness. Instead, he started an antiques business at Nant y Blodau – a business which flourished, and, in no time at all, he was exporting his antiques to all parts of the world.

Around 1850, Newport boasted a total of around twenty-seven public houses, most, if not all of which brewed their own beers. The photograph shows Mr.and Mrs Ernest Davies who later acquired Llys Meddyg. It was his responsibility to travel around the public houses to measure the sugar (and hence the alcohol) content of the beers, and to charge the appropriate duty. He thus became known as 'Davies Excise'. They had two children – Hubert, who became a solicitor at Cardigan and Joyce, who married Captain Cecil Joy, a Master Mariner in the Merchant Navy.

The Llys Meddyg Gardens, *c.* 1948. The *St David* was used as a hospital ship during the Second World War, with Captain Cecil Joy as her master. She assisted with the evacuation from Dunkirk in 1940. After retiring from the Merchant Navy, Captain Joy assisted with the management of the gardens which his wife Joyce had established. These were situated at the eastern approach to Newport and provided employment for a number of the townsfolk. Here Captain Joy is seen with his daughter Jane at the entrance to the gardens.

Upper St Mary's Street, *c.* 1930 looking down from the church chapel. It was at about this time that the telephone service was established in the town, and the exchange was situated a few doors down on the right-hand side. This provided a twenty-four hour service, and it is said that the operators were the best informed citizens of Newport. The large building in the distance is the Ebenezer Congregational chapel.

The opening of the tennis court: The market gardens at Llys Meddyg were extensive in size, and in the middle 1950s, it was decided to build a tennis court at the upper end, which the public could use. These were duly opened by the Mayor in the summer of 1957, and the photograph shows, from left to right: Captain Joy, Air Commodore J.B. Bowen (Lord Lieutenant of Pembrokeshire), Mr.George Evans (Mayor of Newport), Alderman W.J. Jenkins, Alderman W.M. Jermain and Alderman Howard Roberts.

East Street, Newport, *c.* 1920, looking east. The house furthest away is Llys Meddyg (see p.44) and the nearest on the left is Gwalia, where Jack Collings ran his bakery business. Beyond the next house (Cnapan) is the intersection of East Street with Lower and Upper St Mary's Street, and on this corner was installed a water pump from which townsfolk could draw their water supply. It was not until 1938 that water was piped to houses throughout the town.

The Court leet, 1934. Following the crash of an aircraft on Carningli Mountain in August 1934, the co-pilots on board, George Pond and Cesare Sabelli had a remarkable escape. It was extremely fortunate that the plane had landed on 'soft' heather rather than the rock-clad slopes of the mountain. When they had recovered, they were treated like celebrities. Here we see Cesare Sabelli (in the light suit, front) being received by members of the court, the Mayor Alderman Caleb Morris and Lady Lloyd.

High Street Newport Pem, *c.* 1910. This was so called since it was commercially the most important street in the town with premises elegantly called Hellespont House, Manchester House, Le Bon Marche amongst others. It also had a bank, jewellers, and two grocers' shops. The delivery wagon is being reversed towards the premises of J.J. Brown, who provided a daily delivery service of his grocery merchandise throughout the town. The street has since been called Market Street.

Long Street, Newport, *c.* 1906. This is a continuation of Market Street on the lower side of the main road. It is interesting to note that Pullars of Perth (dry cleaners) offered their services at the first house (left-hand side), whilst the next house down was the Angel Temperance Hotel. These premises are now a post office and the newsagent respectively. W. Rowlands is preparing to deliver a load of bread and cakes from the bakery adjacent to his baker's cart.

Bridge Street, Newport, *c.* 1906 is the main street through the centre of the town. In this view looking west towards Fishguard, the Commercial –now the Castle Hotel – stands on the right-hand side. At one time, this was an important staging post for horse-drawn traffic and stage coaches – the stables stand at the end of the pavement. The large building on the left-hand side is the Bethlehem Baptist chapel.

Dressed up for Newport Carnival, 1934. William (Bill) Lewis was appointed to take charge of Barclays Bank in Market Street in 1931. He was an active sportsman who tried to set up a boxing club in the town. However, he was opposed by the chapels who disapproved of 'these pugilistic pursuits'. He then established a local football team which beat the Goodwick brickworks in the final of the North Pembrokeshire Cup at its first time of entering (1935). Here he shows his 'Football Results' at the Carnival.

Milk delivery in Church Street, *c.* 1950. The majority of houses in Newport had their milk supplies delivered to the door by pony and trap until well into the 1970s. There were several suppliers at Newport such as Jack Owen of Cnwce and Dewi Phillips of Bentinck Farm, but here we see Edwards of Pendre who may just have delivered milk to The Great Aunts' Tea Shop (see page 73). He probably then continued into Church Street with some help from his able assistant, Martin Mathias.

Right: Newport Fair, *c.* 1910. There are those living in Newport who still remember the animal sales at Newport, taking place from the Memorial Hall in the west to as far as the Square in the east. Indeed, for many years, the Mayor received 2s 6d for the sale of every horse, 5d per beast, 2d per pig and 1d per stall. Court leet records from 1793 note 'We present Thomas William for buying a horse and not paying the accustomed toll, and therefore we judge the horse as being forfeited to the Lord and Mayor of our Corporation.'

Opposite below: The Barley Mow, seen here in 1908 was one of the public houses in Market Street which survived the attentions of the Temperance Movement. These places were useful not only for slaking one's thirst, but also for the transaction of business. Auctioneers would write to debtors requesting settlement of the debt, using pubs as agreed meeting places, on a given date. The cart outside has brought a consignment of piglets to town for sale in the weekly market in Market Street.

The reopening of St Gurig's Fair, 1950. Ffair Gurig is a long-standing event in the town of Newport, and whilst it was discontinued during the Second World War, it was revived in June 1950 by Dillwyn Miles who was Mayor of the town in that year. Here he is seen flanked by the Mayors of Tenby, Haverfordwest, Pembroke and Cardigan.

Reopening of St Gurigs Fair, 1950. The Mayor of Pembroke thanks the Mayor of Newport Dillwyn Miles, whilst the Bailiff of the Court leet William James stands on the left. It appears that the dodgem cars rink was deemed an appropriate venue for this important speech.

Ffair Gurig in festival year, 1951. The Mayor, John Owen of Cnwce, with Alderman W.M. Jermain (standing left) cuts the tape at the upper end of Long Street, and declares the fair open. The Bailiff William James stands on the right.

Ffair Gurig in festival year, 1951. The Director of Education D.T. Jones, MA, LLB, (nearest the camera) opens the arts and crafts exhibition at the Handicrafts Centre in Newport on 11 July, as part of the Ffair Gurig celebrations. In close attendance are the Mayor, Dillwyn Miles, and Bailiff of the Court leet, William James.

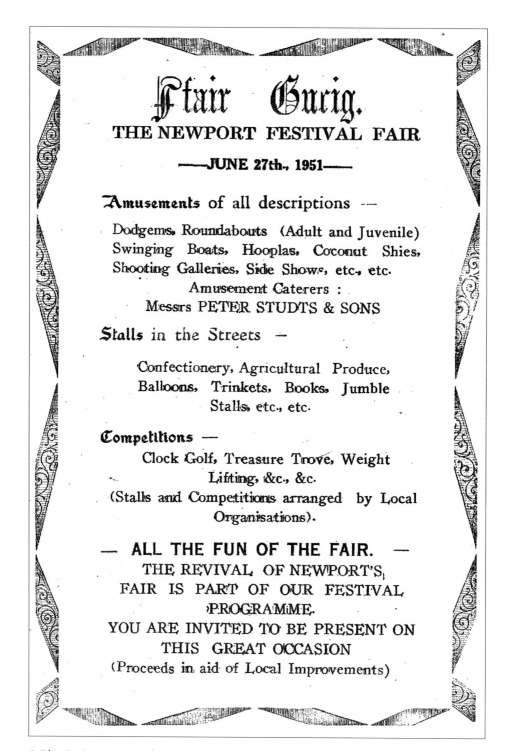

Ffair Gurig.

THE NEWPORT FESTIVAL FAIR

——JUNE 27th., 1951——

Amusements of all descriptions —

Dodgems, Roundabouts (Adult and Juvenile)
Swinging Boats, Hooplas, Coconut Shies,
Shooting Galleries, Side Shows, etc., etc.
Amusement Caterers :
Messrs PETER STUDTS & SONS

Stalls in the Streets —

Confectionery, Agricultural Produce,
Balloons, Trinkets, Books, Jumble
Stalls, etc., etc.

Competitions —

Clock Golf, Treasure Trove, Weight
Lifting, &c., &c.
(Stalls and Competitions arranged by Local
Organisations).

— ALL THE FUN OF THE FAIR. —

THE REVIVAL OF NEWPORT'S
FAIR IS PART OF OUR FESTIVAL
PROGRAMME.
YOU ARE INVITED TO BE PRESENT ON
THIS GREAT OCCASION
(Proceeds in aid of Local Improvements)

A Ffair Gurig programme from 1951. A special effort was made during the Festival of Britain. Apart from all manner of competitions and events spread over the space of four months, and street market stalls, there was a bigger than usual annual fun fair held in the playing field in Long Street.

Programme.

May 23rd—Opening Festival Service at St. Mary's Church, at 7 p.m. Sermon by the Dean of St. Davids (the Very Rev. C. Witton Davies, M.A.).

June 15th— Performance of "Elijah" by the Cardigan Choral Society (Conductor : Andrew Williams, Esq., A.R.C.M.)

June 27th—The Festival Fair.

July 11th—Festival Exhibition at the Newport Handicraft Centre to be opened by D. T. Jones, Esq., M.A., Ll.B., Director of Education for Pembrokeshire.

July 12th.—Visit of Her Royal Highness The Duchess of Kent.
Festival Concert at the Memorial Hall at 7-30 pm

July 25th—Newport Horse Races at Berry Hill Field at 4 pm. Performance of "My Brother George" (Conrad Carter) by the Newport Dramatic Society (Producer : Mrs. J. Jenkins) at the Memorial Hall at 7-30 p.m.

July 27th—Newport Regatta (weather permitting, otherwise August 13th.)
Regatta Dance at Memorial Hall, 8 p.m.—2 a.m.

August 1st—Children's Tea Party on Newport Sands.

August 5th—Community Singing at Parrog at 8 p.m.

August 6th—Bank Holiday Carnival at 3 p.m.
Juvenile Dance at Memorial Hall, 7 p.m.—9 p.m.
Carnival Dance at Memorial Hall, 9 p.m.—2 a.m.

August 8th.—The Mayor's Show and Sports.
Visitors' Concert at Memorial Hall at 8 p.m.

August 15—Festival Ball at Memorial Hall, 9 p m.—2 a.m.

August 22nd—Visitors' Concert at Memorial Hall at 8 p.m.

August 29th.—Cymanfa Ganu (Singing Festival) at Ebenezer Congregational Chapel at 7-30 p.m.

Sept. 4th. & 5th.—Free Church Services.

Sept. 12th—Performance of "Druids Rest" (Emlyn Williams) by the Carningli Repertory Company (Producer : Morton Tucker, Esq., B.A.)

Additional items will be announced later and will include Cricket Matches Golf Tournaments, Eisteddfod, Drama, etc.

Left: Dr H. Bowen Perkins practised as a medical doctor in Newport for many years. He purchased the Prince of Wales public house from the landlord Richard Jackson in around 1865, and rebuilt the property. He also renamed it Llys Meddyg – the Doctor's Court. He was elected Mayor in 1897.

Below: Mr Stephen Evans was elected Mayor for the period 1888-'90. He established a drapery business in Fountain House, Market Street in Newport – a business which survived into the late 1920s.

Opposite: J.O. Vaughan was very much a public man and an entrepreneur in the town. Although he was a ship owner, his primary occupation was as an auctioneer, having his offices, for many years, in West Street. At the time of his installation as Mayor, he hoped that Newport would soon have its own water and sewerage systems, and also electric lighting and tarmacked roads. The previous Mayor had been Dr David Havard, and his mother donated the site for the Memorial Hall. When J.O. Vaughan was elected Mayor in 1920, he grasped the nettle, and the building of the hall commenced and proceeded apace. A hall to remember the dead of the First World War was built and in use by August 1922. The initials of these two gentlemen – JOV and DH – are to be seen on the front of the building as an acknowledgement of their efforts.

The opening of the Memorial Hall. This postcard is the last in a series of three, and the inside of the programme (opposite) indicates that this part of the procession to the Memorial Hall was led by the clergy and ministers Canon D.G. Phillips, the Revd George Morgan and the Revd Ben Morris. They are closely followed by the Ladies' Committee and the children.

The opening of the Memorial Hall, 26 September 1923. The Lord Marcher of the Barony of Cemais, Sir Marteine Lloyd, had preceded that part of the procession shown above, and was accompanied by the-then Mayor of Newport, F.W. Withington. Upon reaching the hall, a silver key was handed to Sir Marteine who then opened the door declaring that the Memorial Hall was officially open.

2—ADDRESS BY CHAIRMAN (F. E. Withington, Esq., J.P.)

3—The Rev. D. G. PHILLIPS, R.D., Rector, will lead the Congregation in repeating the Lord's Prayer.

4—WELSH SCRIPTURE READING by Rev. BEN MORRIS, Ebenezer

5—PRAYER by the Rev. GEORGE MORGAN.

6—The MAYOR will call upon Mr. DAVID RICHARDS to unveil the Memorial Tablet.

7—The names of the Fallen Heroes in the Great War, 1914—1918, will be read by Mr. DAVID RICHARDS. (Audience upstanding).

8—SOUNDING OF THE " LAST POST."

9—HYMN, " Marchog, Iesu, yn llwyddiannus." Tune, "Ebenezer."

Marchog, Iesu, yn llwyddiannus,   Mae Dy enw mor ardderchog,
  Gwisg Dy gleddyf ar Dy glun !   Pob rhyw elyn gilia draw ;
Nis gall daear Dy wrthsefyll,   Mae Dy arswyd trwy'r greadigaeth
  Chwaith nag uffern fawr ei hun ;   Pan y byddot Ti gerllaw.

10—STATEMENT BY THE SECRETARY (Mr. David Thomas).

11—DEDICATION SPEECH by Sir MARTEINE LLOYD, Bart.

12—SHORT ADDRESSES by

Major GWILYM LLOYD GEORGE, M.P.; G. B. BOWEN, Esq., J.P.;
  J. O. VAUGHAN, Esq. (ex-Mayor); Dr. D. HAVARD, M.D.;
    DAVID LUKE, Esq.; Sergt.-Major W. YOUNG DAVIES;
J. LL. HAVARD, Esq.; E. M. DAVIES, Esq.; E. R. GRONOW, Esq.;
  Mrs. VAUGHAN, Hillside, Mrs. Capt. STEPHENS.

13—SOLDIERS' FAVOURITE HYMN, " Cwm Rhondda."

Wele'n sefyll rhwng y myrtwydd   O wrthrychau penna'r byd :
  Wrthrych teilwng o fy mryd :   Ffrynd pechadur,
Er o'r braidd 'rwy'n ei adnabod   Dyma'm llywydd ar y mor.
  Ef uwchlaw gwrthrychau'r byd :   Beth sydd i mi mwy a wnelwyf
    Henffych foreu   Ag eilunod gwael y llawr?
  Caf Ei weled heb un llen.   Tystio'r wyf nad yw eu cwmni
Rhosyn Saron yw Ei enw,   I'w gymharu a'm Iesu mawr :
  Gwyn a gwridog, hardd Ei bryd ;   O, am aros,
Ar ddeng mil y mae'n rhagori   Yn Ei gariad ddyddiau f' oes !

14—BENEDICTION by the RECTOR.

15—DOXOLOGY—

Praise God from Whom all blessings flow,
Praise Him, all creatures here below :
Praise Him above, ye Heavenly host :
Praise Father, Son, and Holy Ghost. Amen.

16—" God Save the King."

Part of the programme for the official opening of the Newport Memorial Hall. Prior to the big event on 26 September 1923, the need for a community hall in Newport had been felt for many years – indeed since before the First World War. The stones from the second storehouse on the Parrog had been donated by E.J. Griffiths of Trewern, and the site had been secured. The foundation stones were laid by Dr Havard and J.O. Vaughan on 1 January 1921. Within a year and a half, the building was ready for use, and was first used for a local Eisteddfod in August 1922. When the foundations for the hall were being opened, the remains of medieval pottery kilns were discovered. Sir Mortimer Wheeler visited the site. Builders were asked to take extra care not to disturb the site. The builders in turn built a room around the pottery. One of the kilns has been preserved .This is now underneath the northern end of the hall and remains intact to this day.

BALANCE SHEET 1st MAY, 1925, TO 1st MAY, 1926.

RECEIPTS.	£	s	d	PAYMENTS.	£	s	d
Balance in hand from last Account	26	1	10	W. H. James—Lavatories, Door, & Painting ...	18	12	0
Proceeds of Bazaar, per Ladies' Committee ...	65	2	0	O. Davies—Painting Windows, Doors, &c. ...	7	12	0
Per Newport (Pem.) United Choir	20	0	0	Williams & Evans—Electric Current, &c. ...	17	19	6
Per Events Committee	20	0	0	G. Aiken—Additional names on Memorial Tablet	2	10	0
Per Eisteddfod Committee	16	12	9	J. Ll. Havard—Automatic Locks for Lavatories,			
Per Library Committee	9	6	3	&c.	7	0	11
Hire of Hall	12	11	0	J. O. Vaughan & D. Luke—Coal	4	13	5
Donations:—				Claim of Ideal Films, Ltd., & Costs ...	2	10	3
Capt. and Mrs. Richards, late of Steeple View	5	0	0	Insurance of Hall Building & Contents	3	1	3
Misses James, London	2	2	0	Duck, Son & Pinker—Attending to Piano ...	0	15	6
Mrs. Griffiths, Cardiff (late of Barley Mow)	1	1	0	Cinematograph & Theatre Licences	0	10	0
Mr. Owen Davies, Delfryn	1	0	0	"County Echo"—Printing	1	5	6
Horticultural Society, Newport (Pem.) ...	1	0	0	Brodog Timber Co.—Battens & Carriage ...	0	8	1
Carningli Branch British Legion	0	10	0	Rates	0	18	4
Balance of Fund re Presentation to Mr. E. M.				Jas. Williams & D. Nicholas—Labour	1	3	0
Davies	2	4	0	Adverse Balance of Library Committee, 1925			
Bank Interest on Deposit Account	1	2	3	Account	0	14	8
Sundries	0	1	3	Lloyd's List for 12 months	3	18	0
Balance due to Bank May 1, 1926	1	1	1	E. J. Riley, Ltd.—for Re-covering Billiard Table	13	7	6
				T. W. Evans—Oilcloth for Billiard Room ...	5	12	0
				12 months' Interest on Memorial Hall Debt to			
				1/5/26	37	10	0
				12 months' Interest on Cinema Debt to 1/5/26	4	8	6
				Repayment of capital to Capt. David Owen ...	25	0	0
				Repayment of part Capital to Capt. John Jones	25	0	0
				Cheque Book	0	5	0
	£184	**15**	**5**		**£184**	**15**	**5**

Audited and found correct.

E. R. GRONOW & J. I. THOMAS, Auditors.

SUMMARY OF ALL RECEIPTS & PAYMENTS SINCE THE COMMENCEMENT OF THE ACCOUNT TO 1st MAY, 1926.

RECEIPTS.	£	s	d	PAYMENTS.	£	s	d
From all sources	4099	11	1	Sundry Payments	3845	12	2
Balance due to Bank 1/5/26	1	1	1	Capital Repaid	255	0	0
	£4100	**12**	**2**		**£4100**	**12**	**2**

CAPITAL ACCOUNT.

	£	s	d
Amount due on Memorial Hall Mortgage May 1925	750	0	0
Repaid Capt. John Jones 1st May, 1926, £25			
Repaid Capt. David Owen 1st May, 1926, £25			
	50	0	0
	£700	0	0
Amount due on Cinema Account May, 1925 ...	88	10	0
Cancelled by Mrs. Lewis, late of Craigymor, 1st May, 1926	1	0	0
	£87	10	0
Amount due on Capital Account 1st May, 1926 £787 10 0			

D. DAVIES.
J. MILTON DAVIES.
Hon. Treasurers.

DAVID THOMAS, Hon. Secretary.

Audited and found correct.

E. R. GRONOW.
J. I. THOMAS.

May 11th, 1926.

This Memorial Hall balance sheet from 1926 gives some idea of the income and running costs for the Memorial Hall. These figures may not seem large to us now, but were substantial sums at that time. The balance sheet also gives us a useful indication, in the receipts column, of the activities carried out at the hall, and the involvement of the local community. The sundry payment on the right would suggest that the cost of the hall was in the order of £4,000.

Gwnewch 180. cards
o'r chai 9/6. Cofiwch
i fod lliain i fod
yn ddrget ai danfon i
mi yn brydue erlyn
y lodge night ynghyd
ynghyd a'r bill.
Yr eiddoch
J. James
Factory
Newport Pem

Industries at Newport in the nineteenth century: This card was written by the manager of a factory at Newport in December 1890. It was addressed to Mr J.C. Roberts, Printer, of Eben's Lane, Cardigan. The half-penny stamp was cancelled, by an E07 Duplex postmark (the number allocated to Newport Pem.), and also a single ring cancellation dated 26 December of that year. It was signed by one J. James, Factory, Newport Pem. Does this mean that this gentleman worked on Boxing Day?

The Benefit Clubs of Newport: The translation of the above card reads 'Would you forward 180 cards of the 9s 6d variety. Remember that there is to be a cloth within – these should be sent to me by the next Lodge Night along with your invoice'.

Prior to the creation of the Welfare State to be out of work meant that there was no income to the household, and that as a result, many families would fall on hard times, a situation further aggravated by sickness and/or bereavement.

Records have subsequently shown that two 'benefit clubs' were established at Newport Pem. The first was the Carningli Lodge of the Ancient Order of Foresters of the Swansea United District. The lodge met at the Commercial (now the Castle Hotel). It was established on the 3 February, 1877 and had a total membership of 135. The secretary of the club was D.O. James, a chemist and photographer from Newport.

The second was The Loyal Kemes Lodge of Oddfellows MU, No. 2488. This lodge met at the Llwyngwair Arms Hotel and was opened on 1 December 1840. It boasted 140 members, and its secretary was John James, of the woollen factory in Newport.

NEWPORT PEM.

Weirglo'r Cnwce and Newport Bay, *c.* 1910. Newport Castle became the home of the Lord Marcher of the Barony of Cemais. He also had bestowed upon him the powers of *jura regalia* – the powers to set up courts to try people for their various offences. Indeed, the citizens of Newport were encouraged to report the wrongdoings and misdeeds of the local populace. Within the walls of the castle there was a gaol for imprisoning criminals and felons of the community until such time as they could be suitably punished. Such punishments might include the stocks or the whipping post, although it is reported in Court leet records in 1720, that this latter item was 'not in working order'.

For extreme offences such as sheep stealing, the Lord Marcher had the power of life and death over the people of the town. The gallows at Newport was situated at Knwc y Krogwith – the mound for hanging, and was situated next to the main road near its junction with Mountain Road West (near the point where this photograph was taken). At this point once stood a farm known as Cnwce. George Owen of Henllys described the area as Warren Tree Lake. In South Pembrokeshire parlance of the time, this meant the gallows or 'Hanging Tree near the stream' (lake). (Note: the place of execution at Cardigan was 'Banc y Warren')

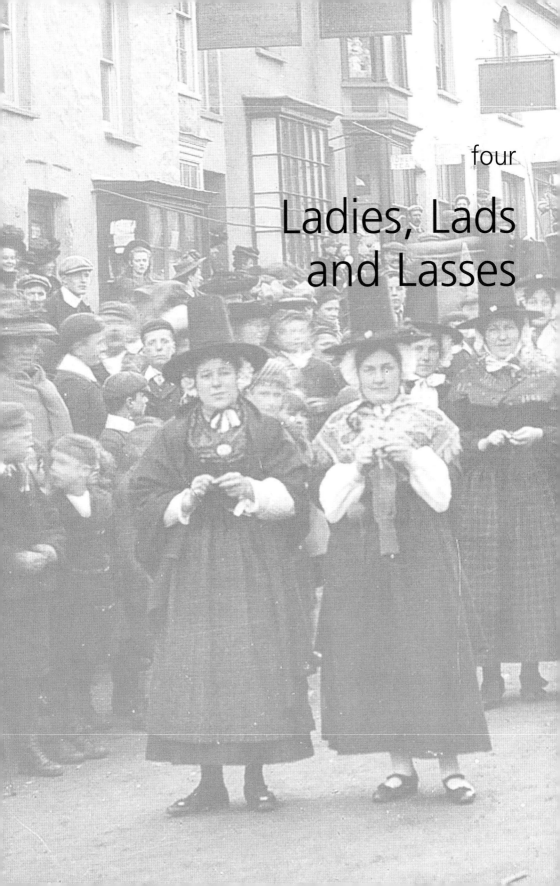

four

Ladies, Lads
and Lasses

The British Women's Temperance Association was established in order to curb the drinking habit throughout the land. In Newport, they helped to reduce the number of public houses and taverns in the town from about twenty-seven in 1850 to a mere fourteen by 1895. They are seen here on their St David's Day march in Market Street in 1908, having just been photographed outside St Mary's church chapel.

A postcard of Newport Castle, Pembrokeshire, postmarked 14 November 1906. Lord Rhys captured the castle at Nevern around 1191. His son-in-law, William Fitz Martin, wanted to secure his sea communications, and thus built himself the castle at Newport, overlooking the estuary of the River Nevern. Following this, he established the garrison town of Novus Burghus (Newburgh, Newport). In turn his son – another William – granted a charter to the town which bestowed many privileges on the burgesses of Newport, rights which are jealously guarded to this day. The castle was the seat of the Lord Marcher of the Barony of Cemais.

The castle, the church and the mill are shown by the eighteenth-century engraver Henry Gastineau, to be in close proximity to one another. Whilst the castle and church are much as indicated, the mill is situated to the right of that depicted. The mill was used for grinding grain, whereas, at about this time, the woollen mills were more important in terms of trade, industry and employment in the area.

St Mary's church at Newport, seen here around 1910, was built at about the same time as the castle – at the beginning of the thirteenth century. The church, dedicated to St Mary the Virgin, is, of itself, unremarkable, and relatively little has been written about it. One of the greatest impacts in the life of the parish was the advent of Methodism in the eighteenth century, and this was sufficient to attract the eminent Methodist preacher, John Wesley, who preached here on at least six occasions.

Above: A postcard of St Mary's church, Newport dated Sept.1914. The photograph shows the interior of the church in the first decade of the last century. The arrangements for the provision of instrumental music up to this time are uncertain, but in 1907, the Vowles organ seen above was installed. Space was a problem, and it was necessary to install the organ in two halves, one half being on each side of the chancel. This caused a loss of light from two windows. The pews in the chancel also had to be shortened to accommodate the instrument. Vowles estimated the total cost at £250.

Right: A Patriotic Fund appeal poster (1854) for the widows and orphans of those killed in the Crimean War. Queen Victoria had been on the throne for only six years before the outbreak of these hostilities in the Middle East.

BARONY of KEMES.

PATRIOTIC FUND.

IN obedience to Her Majesty's Proclama-tion, *Notice is hereby Given*, That a PUBLIC MEETING will be held at NEWPORT, Pembrokeshire, on TUESDAY, the 14th of NOVEMBER instant, at 11 o'Clock in the Forenoon, in aid of the PATRIOTIC FUND, for the RELIEF of the WIDOWS and ORPHANS of SOLDIERS and SAILORS killed in the present War.

LLEWELYN LLOYD THOMAS,
RECTOR OF NEWPORT,

MAYOR.

GOD SAVE THE QUEEN!

Newport Rectory 7th Nov., 1854.

J. POTER, PRINTER, HAVERFORDWEST.

Members of a cookery class at Newport, *c.* 1900. This was sponsored by the late Dr and Mrs David Havard. The young tutor sits between them, and to the right of Mrs Havard (who is holding the boa wrap) is Mrs Evan Jones, the wife of the author of the *Historical Sketch of Newport in Pembrokeshire*. Dr Havard was Mayor of the town from 1876-'78 and it was he who entered into negotiations with the-then county council to pay for half the cost of a new bridge across the River Nevern at Penbont.

Ffair Gurig at Newport Pem., *c.* 1952. Mrs Joyce Joy, along with her daughter Jane promote the produce of Llys Meddyg Gardens outside Pant-Teg at the lower end of Long Street.

Apart from the Girls' Friendly Society, St Mary's church had a strong Sunday school, and those involved in their Christmas pageant in 1952 are shown here. Back row, from left to right: Tommy Rees, Joan Lewis, Eira Isaac, Iris Lindholm, Peggy Lewis. Middle Row: Essex Havard, Revd John Jenkins (elected Mayor in 1953), Charles Watts, -?- , Ron Scriven, Eric Lewis, Mrs Llew Jones, Brian Watts, Granville Varney, -?- , Nigel Drake, Enid Davies, -?- , Leila Griffiths, Cecily Jenkins (producer and wife of Rector), -?- . Front Row: Elizabeth Chessum, Frances Thomas, Helen Drake, Susan Drake, Jane Joy and Gillian Harries. The boys marked -?- are thought to be those who resided at a hostel in Upper St Mary's Street, and may have been evacuees who did not return to London after the war.

Opposite below: The Board school at Newport was established in Lower St Mary's Street following the Education Act of 1870, and opened in 1874. It was further enlarged in 1914 to accommodate 200 children. Its first headmaster was Joshua R. Jones. In its early years, the school population grew to some 150 or so. New regulations demanded that each school should have a Board of Managers. The school provided education for the children of Newport until its closure in 1993 when it was transferred to new modern premises in Long Street.

Madame Bevan's central school. Griffith Jones, the education reformer and Rector of Llanddowror, left his personal fortune to Madame Bridget Bevan for the purpose of establishing circulating schools in North Pembrokeshire. Following her death eighteen years later in 1779, she left £10,000 for the same purpose. Much controversy ensued amongst members of the family regarding the distribution of her assets. It was George Bowen of Llwyngwair, thirty years after this, who finally ensured that the money was used for its intended purpose, and the effort was concentrated on this permanent school, which was named after her.

The St David's Day School Parade in 1916, with many of the children dressed in traditional Welsh costume. The parade is moving along Bridge Street and Cambria Terrace. The young men of the town are noticeable by their absence, and it should be remembered that at about this time, ten per cent of the population of Newport Pem. were away fighting in the First World War.

Newport County primary school, *c.* 1948. This group photograph was taken outside the school. The teacher in charge is Mrs Annie Hughes-Rees, and she herself had lost a son in the Second World War, approximately five years previously. Mrs Hughes was a staunch supporter of the Urdd (Welsh League of Youth) in the town.

The Welsh League of Youth – Urdd Gobaith Cymru – was opened just before the end of the Second World War. These premises were a relic of the First World War, and were not in the best of conditions. They were formally opened in January 1945 by Mr R.E. Griffiths BA, chief organiser of the movement. The building had previously been used by the Newport branch of the Home Guard. The premises were situated on the upper side of Maes Morfa. The two persons who perhaps did most to ensure its success were Miss Mildred Hughes (leader and secretary) and Mrs Annie Hughes Rees (treasurer), a teacher from the primary school.

The Women's Institute stall at Ffair Gurig. Ffair Gurig is still held each year in the town at the end of June, when Long Street is closed to traffic for a morning, and stalls set up by various organisations are laid from the top end of the street down to the car park. Here, the Mayor and Rector of Newport, the Revd John Jenkins collects dues from the WI stall in June 1953.

Left: An advertising card from The Great Aunts tea rooms, *c.*1950. These were situated in the building which had previously been used as a carpenter's workshop at the top end of Market Street.

Market Street, *c.* 1932. Newport Castle appears on the skyline, in front of which stands the building which was used for many years as a carpenter's workshop by Daniel and Benjamin Mathias. On the left-hand side of the street can be seen the building which was once the Barley Mow public house, and next to it, Hellespont House. On the right-hand side is Maescynon, the front room of which was used as the local branch of Barclays Bank Ltd. The proud owner of the Austin 7, which stands outside, was the clerk in charge, Mr Bill Lewis.

Opposite below: The Misses Charlotte and Lucy Glover – the 'Great Aunts' standing outside their tea shop in around 1955. Note the similarity of the adjacent shop sign to the advertising card.

Charlotte and Lucy Glover arrived in Newport early in 1940, having charge of about fifty children evacuated from London during the wartime Blitz. They had responsibility for the education, health and general well-being of these young people. The turmoil created for these youngsters meant that they found it difficult to settle in a country area. This, coupled with the small size of the board school at Newport meant that a special school had to be created for them. This was established at the rear of the Memorial Hall – an ideal situation since all necessary facilities, including a kitchen and sports hall were at hand. Although qualified teachers were employed to teach, both Miss Glovers assisted with these duties. At the cessation of hostilities, the Misses Glover took the children back to London. However, by this time, Newport had 'got into the blood' and within twelve months or so, they both returned and took up residence in The Nook near College Square, realising at the same time that they would need, somehow, to earn a living. They acquired the carpenter's workshop, and after some adaptations, the building was opened as a small café which became known as The Great Aunts tea shop. It existed in this capacity for about fifteen years, and closed in the early 1960s.

Ardent members and supporters of St Mary's church, they both lived well into their eighties and are now interred in the church cemetery.

Newport, Pembs. Women's Institute

Programme for 1958.

President : Mrs. A. HUGHES-REES.

Vice-Presidents : Mrs. G. ROBERTS; Mrs. LLEW. JONES; Mrs E. CHESSUM.
Hon. Treasurer : Mrs. M. HARRIES; Hon. Secretary : Mrs. D. THATCHER.
Asst. Treasurer : Miss M. RICHARDS; Deputy Secretary : Mrs. T. JENKINS.

Committee :— Mrs. EDWARDS; Mrs. GRIFFITHS; Mrs. T. JENKINS; Mrs N.
LEWIS; Mrs. LOCKLEY; Miss M. RICHARDS; Co-opted : Mrs.
MOSTYN-DAVIES; Miss EVANS, Maesycurig; Mrs. MACNAMARA.

"Home and Country" : Mrs. LLEW. JONES. Tea Secretary : Mrs. T. JENKINS.
Produce Guild Secretary : Mrs. G. ROBERTS. Press Corresp. : Mrs. HUGHES REES

MEETINGS are held unless otherwise stated, on the SECOND WEDNESDAY of
each month in the READING ROOM, MEMORIAL HALL at 2.30 p.m.

JANUARY 8th. :

Film Show and Talk by
Mr. A. Davies.
Comp. : Best Nylon Flower.
Tea Hostesses :
Mrs Edwards; Mrs. Griffiths; Mrs.
Hughes.

January 15th.: Whist Drive, 7.30 pm.

FEBRUARY 12th. :

Cookery Demonstration by
Mrs. G. Roberts.
Comp. : Best Cornish Pasty.
Tea Hostesses :
Miss Evans, Maesycurig; Mrs Evans
Awelfa; Mrs. George, Brigydon.

February 19th. : Open Meeting :
Talk and Film Show on Northern
Ireland by the Northern Ireland
Publicity Representative. 7-30 pm.

MARCH 12th. :

Demonstration of Painting on
China and Glass by
Cepea Products (Trichem)
Comp. : Best Fancy Coathanger.
Tea Hostesses:
Mrs Harries; Mrs Hughes-Rees;
Mrs. Llew. Jones.

March 13th. and 14th. :
County Sugar Work Schools.

Wednesday, March 19th. : Sale of
Work at 2-30 p.m.

APRIL 9th. :

Talk on Education by
County Education Officer.
Comp. : Best Arrangement of
Flowers in an Egg-cup.
Tea Hostesses :
Mrs. John, Prendergast;
Mrs. Lewis, Morfa; Mrs. Lockley.

SPRING GROUP MEETINGS
Date not yet fixed.

MAY 14th. :

Talk by Mrs. V. Morgan on
Holidaying in Ireland in a Gipsy
Caravan.
Comp : Prettiest Nightie (Home-
made or other).
Tea Hostesses:
Mrs. Mc Bride; Mrs Mathias, Mill;
Mrs. Mendus.

JUNE 11th. :

OUTDOOR MEETING : Treasure
Hunt to Nevern.
Comp. : Best Bunch of Wild Flowers
Picked on way.
Tea Hostesses :
Miss Payn; Mrs Partridge;
Nurse Price.

JULY 9th. :

Probably Open Meeting—Details
later.
Comp. : Best Home-made Necklace.
Tea Hostesses :
Mrs. Thomas, Westleigh; Mrs. H.
Roberts; Mrs. G Roberts.

AUGUST—No Meeting.

SEPTEMBER 10th. :

Cookery Demonstration by
Wales Gas Board.
Comp : Best Miniature Wild Flower
Arrangement.
Tea Hostesses:
Mrs. Thatcher; Miss Richards
Miss Turner.

Week beg. September 29th :
AUTUMN GROUP MEETINGS

OCTOBER 9th. THURSDAY

Making Felt Hats by
Mrs. I. Davies Haverfordwest.
Comp. : Best Old Plate.
Tea Hostesses :
Mrs. Williams, Bronmor;
Mrs. Havard; Mrs Mathias, Cambria

NOVEMBER 5th. :

County Three Year Work Exhibition

November 11th. : Annual Meeting
Comp. : Ankle Judging.
Tea Hostesses:
Mrs. Joy; Mrs. Phillips, Aber' we;
Mrs. Jones, Glendale.

DECEMBER 10th. :

Talk by the Fire Service on
Fire Prevention in the Home.
Comp. : Best Mince Pie.
Tea Hostesses :
Mrs June Jones; Mrs. Morris;
Mrs. Parry.

The Annual Outing will be held
about June 21st., and a Christmas
Party during December or early
January.

If you are unable to take your turn
as Tea Hostess, please find substi-
tute. Mrs Jenkins has list.

A Newport Women's Institute programme poster for 1958. This reflects the breadth of interest, frequency of meetings and the involvement of individuals in the institute. By this time, membership had exceeded fifty, about twenty-five per cent of whom served as officers or committee members.

Newport carnivals are usually held in the month of July. With the establishment of the second Women's Institute group in April 1968, a friendly rivalry developed between the two institutes as to who could produce the best float. Both floats seen here are from around 1970. Above, from left to right: Mrs Major Lewis, Lit Lewis, Norah Roberts, Eileen Buchanan, Nansi Lewis, Thora Jenkins. Front row: Muriel Phillips, Mary Richards, Eileen McBride, Dora Thatcher and Sally Davies. Ugunde's wives include Joan Evans and Rosemary Scarr.

In 1968, the joint Women's Institute theatrical group staged a performance of *The Brilliant and the Dark*: an operatic sequence for women's voices commissioned by the National Federation of Women's Institutes. The work was composed by Malcolm Williamson and performed in more than fifty counties throughout the land. Sir Marcus Dodds adjudicated these performances – not small task – and selected the best for the national performance of the work at the Royal Festival Hall in June 1969. Members of Newport and Carningli Women's Institutes took part in the Pembrokeshire production held at the County Theatre, Haverfordwest.

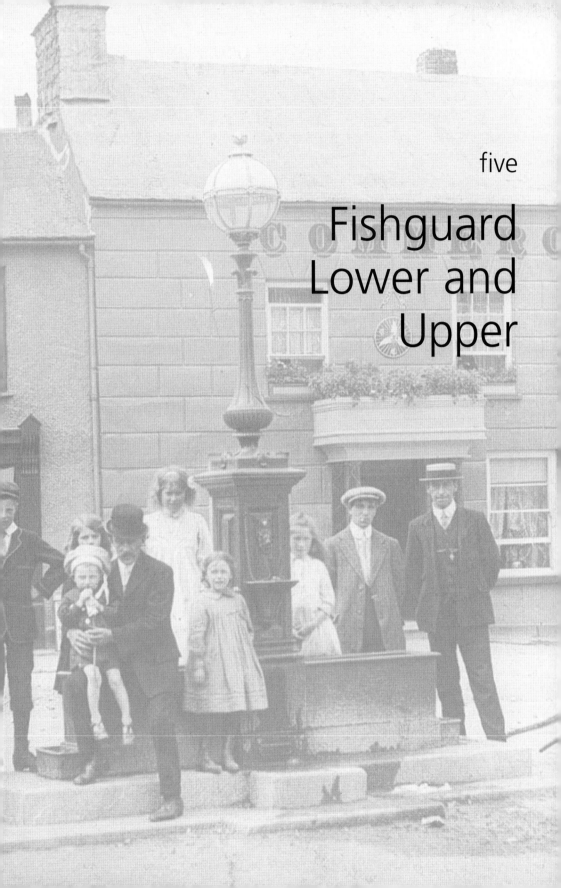

five

Fishguard Lower and Upper

The fort at Fishguard: At the end of the eighteenth century, privateers had an unpleasant habit of raiding townships, and Fishguard, being the third largest town in Pembrokeshire at the time, was a prime target. After a great deal of persuasion, the Ordnance Board reluctantly allowed Fishguard a fort, and this was completed in 1781. When a scouting party of the French invasion fleet entered the harbour in 1797, all the militia could do was to fire one of their three rounds of ammunition. Fortunately, the party turned and fled, declaring that Fishguard was 'heavily defended'.

Harbour facilities at Lower Fishguard, c. 1905 The harbour was very busy up to this time, particularly when the tides were high. Records indicate that in 1795, there were about fifty ships which called regularly at the port, trading principally with Bristol. Main imports included coal, culm and limestone, and exports included dairy products, grain, locally quarried slate and an abundance of herring.

The harbour at Lower Fishguard is much quieter than previously, mainly because of the arrival of the railway and the new harbour on the western side of the bay. Imports had to be carried from Lower Fishguard, and the hills to be climbed to Fishguard or Newport were very steep. The message on this card, postmarked 1 December 1913 reads 'I am sending you the photo of the new hill opened last week'.

The opening of the new road, on 25 November 1913. The new road was a great acquisition for Fishguard. Above, we see the Mayor's Wolseley car approaching the tape. This was the first vehicle to be driven along the new road. In attendance were the Mayor, local councillors and other civic dignitaries.

The bridge at Lower Town (postmarked 1916) was built and opened in 1875, and replaced a four-arched stone-built structure. On the highest tides, fairly large trading vessels could come up river to this point, and flour from Grace Bros. of Bristol was discharged into the large warehouse situated just to the left of this picture up until 1929. The building has since been used by the Sea Scouts of TS (Training Ship) *Skirmisher*.

Fishguard Bay in the post-war years. The vessels in the harbour, from left to right are: *St Patrick*, *Great Western* and *St David*. The breakwater railway siding is full of cattle wagons. The postcard is dated 18 August 1954, and the message reads 'Film stars here making *Moby Dick*, but too wet to be out today, so no autographs'. The barges (centre left) were used during the filming. The film starred the late Gregory Peck.

The industries at the Slade. In the left foreground can be seen the ubiquitous limekilns, which are situated at most inlets and bays around the coast. About two hundred yards above this was the timber yard run by J.M. Guild, no doubt useful for the shipbuilding and repair. The message reads 'Just a line to let you know that I came home quite sober – don't forget the Keens like rabbits'. The postcard is dated 1915. Ironically, Mr Guild was killed by a falling tree.

From the Slade to the town, *c.* 1910. Mr Guild's timber yard can be seen at the bottom right in this photograph, as the road winds up a steep hill to the town. A terrace of houses can be seen on the skyline. The houses which now stand on the remainder of the skyline are conspicuous by their absence in this photo. The Gorsedd Circle has been built some 100 yards to the right of this point.

Main Street, Fishguard, 1902 (top) and 1915 (bottom). The street was so called because it was the principal road leading from the upper (new) town to the lower (old) town. The first building on the left was the original home of the Baptist movement in Fishguard which later became the Great Western Hotel. Beyond the Cambridge House Restaurant (with its 'Well Air'd Beds'), Bowen's Tea Rooms and Nicholas' Cycle & Motor Depot can all be seen.

Pentowr Sunday school, 1948. Pentowr chapel stands about 100 yards from the top of the Fishguard /Lower Town hill, and is the home of the Methodists and Presbyterians. On Sundays, services were held in the morning and evening, with Sunday school in the afternoon. The high point of the year was the Sunday school trip, when there would be sufficient adults and children (from one chapel) to fill three buses. The leaders of the School were Mr J.J. Morgan (centre) and Mrs E.D. Evans (right).

Furlong's taxi depot, c. 1905. Controversy has been generated regarding the location of depots. This one was behind the Great Western Hotel in Main Street. It was owned by the Furlong Brothers George and Tom (wearing white hats). Will Thomas (with the whip) – the father of Mr Edgar Thomas – was a driver, foreman and carpenter for the company. He earned a weekly wage of £5 – good money in those days. At one time they owned Furlong's Hotel.

Fishguard Square, *c.* 1914. This magnificent photograph shows the Commercial Hotel prior to the time it was restyled and renamed the Abergwaun Hotel. Standing alongside is Martin's shop which was both a newsagent and stationers – a business which was to remain buoyant under the charge of the sisters Hilda and Vida until the mid 1950s. Hilda taught for some time at the local primary school.

Fishguard Square. This card is postmarked September 1913. In 1853, the inhabitants of Fishguard raised sufficient money by subscription to purchase the gardens which once stood where The Square is now. The Square is, geographically and commercially at the centre of the town. In this image, at the near left stands the Farmers' Arms, and next to it, Griffiths' Castle grocery stores.

Fishguard Square, *c.* 1955. This scene is much changed from the last. The Commercial Hotel has been rechristened, and the Square is fairly busy. Norman Llewellyn of Maesgwyn can be seen here, still using a pony and cart to deliver milk. At one time, the cart carried a heavy brass-banded milk churn with a tap at its base, and milk was measured into a container of known capacity. It was only when he was certain that your jug held no more than the amount requested, that the milk was measured directly into your jug.

Fishguard Square, *c.* 1980. In an Act of Parliament of 1834, permission was granted to the people of Fishguard to build a market hall, (at their own expense), and the money was raised by selling £5 shares, limiting the purchase by any individual to twenty. In addition to this, donations were received from Sir John James and Lady Hamilton, and also from J.H. Phillips, the local Member of Parliament.

Mauretania Day at Fishguard.

FISHGUARD
MARKET HOUSE 1836

Tolls payable pursuant to an Act of Parliament
Passed in the fourth year of William the IV   27th June 1834

	L	s	d
For every imperial bushel of wheat, not exceeding........................			1½d
" " " " " oats & other grain & seeds..............			1d
For storage of every imperial bushel of corn, grain & seed from one market day to another...			0½d
For every stall used by a butcher for selling flesh, meat being actually his own property, inclusive of weighing & toll, not not exceeding by the day		1s	3d
by the year...............	3	3s	0d
For every half stall, with joint use of, by the day			9d
" " " " , " " " " , " " year........................	1	10s	0d
For every basket with butter, poultry, rabbits, game & wildfowl, fish, plants, vegetables & roots, not exceeding			2d
For every superficial foot for holding earthenware & pottery....			1d
" " " " holding sacks & bags containing roots vegetables and other articles			1d
For every imperial bushel of potatoes, turnips, carrots & other roots sold in carts not exceeding..			½d
For every cartload of cabbage plants, not exceeding...................		1s	6d
For every Showman's Wagon, not exceeding by the day..........		10s	0d
For every Showman's Cart, not exceeding by the day		2s	6d

N.B. Caution to any Person or Persons hawking their goods about the town, and any persons purchasing the same will be subject to the penalties stated in the Act of Parliament for same,

Above: Mauretania Day. This postcard dated 1909 reflects the euphoria felt following the inauguration of the Cunard service at Fishguard Harbour. This optimism lasted many months. This photograph, taken from the first floor of the market hall shows the celebrations on Fishguard Square. The populace was bedecked in bibs, bonnets and boaters, whilst the lifeboat men can be seen standing to attention wearing their cork life jackets.

Left: Stall holders' tariff list, Fishguard Market, 1836. Prior to this date, market traders could only sell their wares and produce on the streets of the town, and this they had to do, winter or summer, rain or shine. The hall was opened in 1836 at an estimated cost of £1,800. The tariff for stall holders remains in the market hall to this day, and there was a stern warning for those who might persist with the old practices (see note at bottom of list).

Fishguard Square, 14 October 1932. The GWR Road Service buses, which had travelled from Fishguard and Goodwick station to Cardigan since 1920, were replaced in 1928 by the Western Welsh Omnibus Co., one of whose vehicles can be seen on the 'wrong' side of the road beyond Barclays Bank on the left. Fishguard Square is busier than usual, for the church dignitaries have been present for the laying of the foundation stones at the St Mary's church Institute (opposite the tree) on this same date.

Fishguard High Street, *c.* 1910 was the main arterial route to Haverfordwest, and used, at one time, by nearly all traffic to and from Fishguard Harbour. The young lady to the left stands at the entrance to the Messrs. Furlong's other taxi depot, and Fishguard Square lies just beyond the houses at the far end of the street.

Fishguard County primary school, *c.* 1949. Opened on 6 October 1909 by Lady St Davids, it had separate entrances for boys and girls. The teachers generally were loved by the children, in particular Miss Myrtle Richards (pictured) and Miss Haiddwen Jones, who had been a tutor to the Queen and Princess Margaret. Miss Richards had the special responsibility for preparing children for the Scholarship Examination (later known as the Eleven Plus), and children were constantly warned by the somewhat tyrannical headmaster that unless they worked hard, they would end up 'weeding Larcombe's cabbages'.

West Street, Fishguard, seen here around 1900, is now very much different from how it appeared here. Here it is viewed from the hill at the end of Penslade. The Slade runs down on the left. The two nearest cottages and walls in the foreground have since been demolished. The council school was built on the other side of the tallest building (the bakery at Goodwick House).

West Street, Fishguard from Vergam Terrace, *c.* 1916: At the near left was situated Fishguard's second post office. Postmaster W. Eynon published this card, and from the garage (next door but one), Christmas Evans ran his taxi service. The building beyond the two ladies is the former Temperance Hall, used by the school in 1895, and Mr Strawbridge later established his bakery where Oliver's shoe shop is in this picture, on the near right corner.

Clive Road, Fishguard, leads from the join of West Street and Vergam Terrace, and comprises rows of terrace houses on each side of the road. At the entrance was Mr Strawbridge's shop, where the best bread in town could be bought. At the top end of the road stood the market gardens of Mr Ivor J. Larcombe, beyond which stands the old county school. This postcard is dated 1915.

The Proclamation Ceremony. Each year, the Royal National Eisteddfod of Wales is held in a different part of the country, normally alternating between the north and the south. This is always preceded by a proclamation ceremony – where a declaration of intent is made that the Eisteddfod will come to that place. In this image, the procession is making its way to the Gorsedd Circle, on 27 July 1935.

A publicity envelope created for the 1936 Eisteddfod at Fishguard.

The Royal National Eisteddfod of Wales was held at the town of Fishguard on the 3-8 August 1936. The preparation was thorough, and fundraising was so successful that income for the event exceeded expenditure by a sum of £1,200. It was said at the time that 'the Ladies in Red Shawls' were as ready for the 'Invasion' as their forbears had been for the French invasion of 1797, but it was likely that the reception would be less hostile!

Most households in Fishguard at the time were Welsh speakers, and it is estimated that more than ninety per cent of these offered accommodation for visitors and competitors. The opening ceremony was performed by Sir Evan Jones (Eisteddfod Chairman) and Major Gwilym Lloyd George MP, and was attended by about 15,000 people – a number far too large to be accommodated in the Eisteddfod Pavilion. On stage were their wives, Alderman and Mrs Fred Evans (Mayor and Mayoress of Cardiff), and Mr and Mrs W.L. Williams, Cefn y Dre. The event was visited by David Lloyd George on the Thursday of Eisteddfod week.

Things did not run quite according to plan, since halfway through the Guest of Honour's address, the loudspeakers broke down. Those left outside the Pavilion could not hear, and there was much unrest. The guest speaker was stopped in his tracks. Following an appeal from the Chairman, order was restored, as were the loudspeakers, following which the crowds were satisfied and went home.

Opposite below: The Gorsedd Circle. A circle of twelve stones was created for the event with the logan stone at its centre, where the Archdruid stood to make the proclamation. Seen here is the circle used at Fishguard in 1935. On each of the stones was carved the name of the village which donated it. A second Gorsedd Circle was created at Lota Park, to facilitate the ceremony for the 1986 Eisteddfod.

Fishguard County school. The original school was started in 1895 at the Temperance Hall (now Theatre Gwaun) with forty-three pupils. After one year, Owen Gledhill was appointed as Headmaster. With rapidly increasing pupil numbers, there was a chronic shortage of space. This was partly overcome when the new school, shown here, was built on Ropewalk Hill around 1901, at a cost of £1,416 with a further £209 for the provision of equipment.

Fishguard Bay Regatta, 1905. The great day in August had arrived. The large vessel in the middle is the Umpires' boat, and it is very likely that Tom Furlong (see pg 83) is aboard. When he was not taking part in the regatta, he was a trainer of boxers. The longboat rowing tradition, where four crew and a coxswain man the boat, is strong in North Pembrokeshire, and none more so than at Fishguard. Here, the longboats gather, all ready for the race.

The Fishguard Bay Regatta was paid for by public subscription. Here, hundreds have gathered to view the competitions from their vantage points overlooking the old harbour at Lower Town. To win a competition was a matter of prestige, and carried significant prizes. The crowds are dressed in their Sunday best for the occasion.

The wreck of the *Evviva*, 1895. The *Evviva* was a Norwegian barque carrying a load of timber from Scandinavia to Bristol. She was caught in a violent storm, and her sails were torn to ribbons by the time she reached south Cardigan Bay. She was totally out of control and it was thought that she might be wrecked on the Cow and Calf rocks. With a change in wind direction she was eventually destroyed on the rocks at Saddle Point, scattering her cargo throughout the bay.

Windy Hill, Fishguard 1914. This is the last Fishguard street one would encounter en route when travelling to Goodwick. At the far end of the street were a number of houses retained for the exclusive use of the local coastguards, whilst at the near left (out of shot) stands the local Masonic lodge. The message reads 'the pony and trap will drive you back Wensday [sic] morning if that will do.'

Bridge over the River Drim, *c.* 1912. This more or less formed the boundary between Fishguard and Goodwick. The river is tidal up to the bridge and beyond, and the marsh through which it flowed was an ideal spot for catching eels. On the skyline (top left), St Theresa's Convent and Rest Home for the aged can be seen.

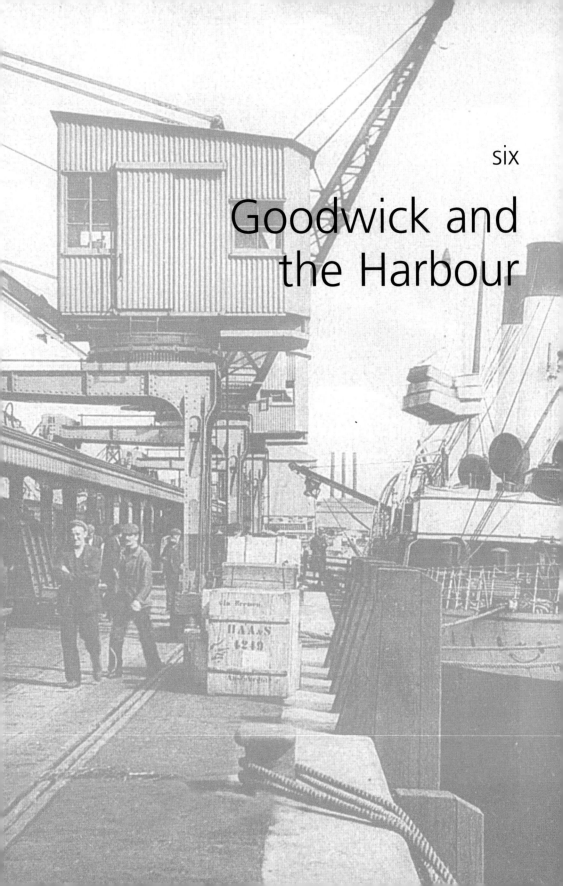

six

Goodwick and the Harbour

The Promenade at Goodwick was the 'place to be' at the beginning of the last century. Seen here in 1905, a fashionable young couple take the fresh air near the beach at Parrog. Berachah chapel was under construction at this time; in anticipation of an influx from Neyland, the railway had reached Goodwick, and Mr Furlong's horse-drawn taxi can be seen taking a passenger from the station to Fishguard.

The approach to Fishguard station, *c.* 1908. As this image shows, the station is well established at this point. Indications are that most of the traffic was still horse-drawn, and the railway line has been built through to the harbour, which opened two years previously. Fishguard and Goodwick station, as it later became known, was the bus terminus for the Cardigan services (via Newport) which were run by Mr Howard Roberts and the Western Welsh Omnibus Co.

The Promenade at Goodwick, *c.* 1907. As seen here, the area was enhanced with a beautiful stone wall. $3\frac{1}{2}$ million tons of rock were removed from the distant cliff to provide the twenty-seven acres occupied by the new harbour. At this time, the main approach to the harbour was by way of the Fishguard Bay Hotel – the road can be seen at the base of the cliff.

Main Street, Goodwick, *c.* 1906. The impact of the railway had not quite hit Main Street at this point, and business was relatively undeveloped. The writer of the postcard recorded that 'We had a pleasant evening last Wednesday in Fishguard as General Booth was giving a lecture on the Past, Present & Future. It was very good.'

Visits to Goodwick Beach, 1908 and 1950. It is interesting to note that in the first decade of last century, people would dress up to go to the beach. The visitors in the earlier picture are thought to have been on a church outing from Little Newcastle. The north breakwater is almost complete. Some forty years later, the dress for the beach is distinctly casual. The beach is very safe with water encroaching slowly over a large flat area of sand.

Main Street, Goodwick in 1930. Trees had been removed and a row of shops established along the right-hand side of the street. The Welcome Chip Bar was on the left. Motorised transport was taking over. Fishguard's main police station was situated just to the right of the photo, and at times up to thirty police officers were based here.

Public transport in North Pembrokeshire, *c.* 1930. The Great Western Railway ran its bus service from Fishguard and Goodwick station to Cardigan, from July 1920 to the end of July 1929. Thereafter, it sold its local fleet to the Western Welsh Omnibus Co., who continued the service until around 1960. Although the Fishguard to Cardigan route was served by AEC and Maudslay ML3 buses, a number of the above Thornycroft 'A1' vehicles were allocated to operate from Cardigan.

The lifeboat service at Fishguard was established in 1822 with its first vessel being built locally at a cost of £95. *The Elizabeth Mary* (above) was, in effect, a reserve lifeboat which cost £300, and was in service between 1889 and 1907. She was manned by a ten-man crew – with ten oars – along with the coxswain James Thomas. When the call came, she would be drawn by horses from No.1 station (near to the railway station and the present day Stena Line reception office) and reversed into the water.

The building of Harbour Village, *c*. 1905. The decision by the GWR to transfer their ferry service to Ireland from Neyland to Fishguard presented major logistical problems for the company. Existing housing stock was grossly inadequate to absorb the workforce which would be transferred from Neyland. Here, the building programme at Harbour Village has begun.

Goodwick, St Davids Place.

St David's Place, Goodwick, *c.* 1910. The GWR in effect, built two villages: one at Harbour Village, and at St David's Place. The situation at the former enabled the workers to walk down the hillside to the harbour, a walk of ten minutes or so, whilst the latter was located in close proximity to the locomotive depot at Goodwick. Workers could thus be called at short notice in the event of an emergency.

The original fisherman's quay at Goodwick presented a major obstacle for the GWR in its planning of facilities at Fishguard Harbour. Fishermen had long before this, established their own quay at the waterside, near to the location of the Fishguard Bay Hotel. Fishermen were concerned that they would be deprived of their livelihoods. Following negotiations the fishermen were persuaded to move further south.

The 'new' fisherman's quay at Goodwick. In return for their cooperation, the GWR built the fishermen the quay wall, shown here with their boats tied alongside. The Brixham trawler fleet, from Cornwall, is visible further out in the bay, preparing to depart.

St Peter's church and the bay, *c.* 1908. The construction of the inner breakwater is well advanced in this photograph, with ballast-carrying railway wagons half way along. On the waterfront beyond the church tower, the 'pell mell' block works (forty-ton blocks of concrete) are being manufactured. These will then be placed on the north side of the outer (north) breakwater by *Titan*, the crane.

Opposite below: Fishguard and Goodwick station, *c.* 1955. The tower breaking the skyline belongs to St Peter's church, and the chimney is that of Goodwick brickworks. The houses at the base of the chimney are those of St David's Place. In its heyday, the morning train would travel to the Trecwn armaments depot, and local trains to Rosebush and Clarbeston Road, as well as express passenger and heavy goods trains to and from the harbour.

The locomotive depot at Fishguard, *c.* 1946. Up until the building of the harbour, the station at Goodwick was used only by tank engines or rail motors. These could travel forwards or backwards, and so the establishment of a locomotive depot with turning and other sophisticated facilities was not necessary. However, with heavy goods and passenger engines travelling further afield, the situation changed.

The depot, built to the standard G.J. Churchward design, was opened in 1906. It had an engine shed (centre left) which could house four locomotives, and it was here that the general repair and maintenance took place. Typically, a train would arrive at the harbour, the locomotive would be uncoupled, and run in reverse to the depot (approximately $1\frac{1}{2}$ miles). Here it would be washed and polished, turned on the turntable and coaled and watered from the coaling stage on the right before being returned to service at the harbour.

Every engine shed had an allocation of locomotives. Fishguard had fifteen. The largest engines allocated to this depot were numbers 4982 Acton Hall, 5905 Knowsley Hall, 5928 Haddon Hall and 6823 Oakley Grange. It had a further six Pannier tanks (for local running and shunting), and five 14xx class auto-tanks for local passenger running. With the demise of steam locomotion and the advent of the diesel locomotive, the depot was, sadly, closed in 1963.

Fishguard Harbour engineering workshops and stores, *c.* 1908. The main workshop was that nearer the water. A further workshop and stores were housed in the adjacent building. The power house was to the left of these buildings (just out of shot). This provided electrical power for the dockside cranes, lighting for the harbour buildings including the Fishguard Bay Hotel, as well as for workers' houses at Harbour Village. This was a very advanced development at this time.

Fishguard Harbour engineering workshops, *c.* 1908 provided a very comprehensive engineering service with blacksmiths, copper and tinsmiths, millers, lathe operators and engineering fitters. It provided a general repair service for the ships. In the foreground can be seen a marker buoy, and in the centre, a ship's propeller. These items were frequently required particularly when ships sailed in shallow water, for example, the Waterford River.

Fishguard Bay Hotel, *c.* 1920. By the time of this photograph, the hotel's hopes for glory had diminished. However, the grounds remained beautiful, with palm trees and tennis courts, and the hotel still provided for those passengers wishing to break their journey en route to Ireland. This continued until around 1960.

AN entirely new Hotel, with every modern convenience.

Ideally situated, over-looking the magnificent Harbour and surrounding country.

A delightful place to stay at after an Ocean voyage, en route to or from Ireland or for a summer or winter holiday.

Sub-tropical Gardens of great extent and beauty.

Complete electric lighting. Telephones in every room.

Excellent Cuisine.

An advertising card for the Bay Hotel from around 1912. The GWR extolled the facilities that were available, and other documentation boasted such luxuries as the 'electric lifts to all floors'. The elegance of the hotel can still be enjoyed today as little has changed internally. With the 'roll on, roll off' facilities of the ferry, and rapid transit of passengers, it is the clientele that has changed, and the premises are now often used for weddings and conferences.

Great Western Railway steamers at Fishguard in 1906. To provide the cross-Channel service, the GWR purchased three new steamers; the *St David*, the *St George* and the *St Patrick*, all similar in design to that shown above. The *St Andrew* was acquired two years later. The ships were of 2,500 tons displacement, and each had a speed capability of eighteen knots. The *St George* was sold to the Canadian Pacific Railway Company in 1912, but despite this, she became a hospital ship at the outbreak of hostilities.

Irish Ferries at Fishguard, 1906. Ferry services were provided, not only to Rosslare, but also to Cork and Waterford. The latter service was retained following an agreement with the Irish authorities when the service was transferred from Neyland to Fishguard. The City of Cork Steam Packet Company's *Inniscarra* (above) was the very first ship to use the completed terminal.

The replacement ships at Fishguard in 1932 were also named the *St David*, *St Patrick* and *St Andrew*, and were similar in design to that shown here. At the outbreak of the Second World War, the *St David* and the *St Andrew* were commandeered for wartime service, and, whilst the *St David* was lost at Anzio, ironically, the ship left at home, the *St Patrick* (below) was bombed and sunk twelve miles off Strumble Head. The *St David* served at Dunkirk under Captain Cecil Joy.

R. M. S. St. Patrick.

G.W.R. Steamboat Arrangements for Bank Holiday
2nd August 1909

Steamboat Departures from and Arrivals at Fishguard

S.S. St.Andrew: - *Isle of Man Excursion. Leave Fishguard 1.45 am Monday arrive Douglas 8.15am. Leave Douglas 9.00am arrive Fishguard 3.30 am Friday*

S.S. St. George: - *Killarney, Oroca (?) & Dublin Excursion. Leave Fishguard 2.40 am Monday. Arrive Rosslare 5.25 am. Leave Rosslare 11.50 pm to arrive at Fishguard 2.35 am Friday*

S.S. St.David: - *Ordinary Mailboat. Leave Fishguard 2.25 pm Arrive Rosslare 5.55 pm . Leave Rosslare 12.15 am arrive Fishguard 3.10 am Tuesday*

S.S. St.Patrick: - *Ordinary Mailboat. Leave Rosslare 1.00 pm arrive Fishguard 3.55 pm. Leave Fishguard 2.35 am arrive Rosslare 5.35 am Tuesday*

S.S. Great Western:) *Leave Fishguard 11.45 pm arrive Waterford 8.00 am*
S.S. Pembroke:) *Leave Waterford 5.35 pm arrive Fishguard 4.00 am Daily Sundays excepted.*

S.S. Inniscarra: - *Leave Fishguard 11.25 pm Saturday arrive Cork 9.25 am Sunday. Leave Cork 7.25 pm Monday arrive Fishguard 5.30 am Tuesday*

S.S. Sir Francis Drake: *Leave Fishguard 11.00 am for 2 hour cruise to the Westward.*
Leave Fishguard 2.30 pm for cruise around Ramsay Is About 4 hours
Leave Fishguard 7.00 pm for 2 hour cruise to the North Eastward

With a substantial investment in the harbour and its ships, the GWR were determined that assets were not to lie idle, even at Bank Holiday times. This information is taken from publicity material of the time. It is interesting to note that the Sir Francis Drake, a passenger and mail tender for the Cunard Liners, had arrived at Fishguard more than a month before the arrival of the *Mauretania*.

Opposite below: The crowds view the activity from immediately above the harbour. The passengers were landed at the main harbour whereas passengers' luggage was landed at the Atlantic Wharf – a terminal specially erected for the purpose. The breakwater was decorated with bunting, and *Titan* the crane remained busy with construction work at the end of the breakwater.

Fishguard, R.M.S. Mauretania.

The Arrival of the *Mauretania* in 1909. To further justify their investment in Fishguard Harbour, the GWR had long held ambitions for involvement with the Cunard Line and the Trans-Atlantic trade. Their dreams were realised on 30 August with the arrival of the *Mauretania* – the largest and fastest vessel afloat, and holder of the prestigious Blue Riband. Thousands turned out to see her, all dressed in their Sunday finery.

R.M.S. Mauretania off Fishguard Breakwater.

Industrial unrest at Fishguard Harbour, 1911. The staff at Fishguard Harbour went on strike for more pay in 1911. The GWR were eager to settle rather than run the risk of disrupting the Cunard Line traffic. Shortly after the settlement however, there was a call for a national strike which the Fishguard men joined. At this stage the army was called in, and here they can be seen billeted in the Marsh sidings.

The troops at play on Goodwick Beach, 1912. There are those who contend that the soldiers sent to Fishguard were of the Royal Sussex Regiment, but judging by the men entering the water, there is not much to go on!

The arrival of the *Mauretania,* 1909. The big ship has just arrived, and it is clear from the above postcard that both passengers and mails were discharged to a single tender, in this case the *Sir Francis Drake.* 'Turn around' time for the big liners was between forty-five and sixty minutes, during which alighting passengers, all their luggage and mail bags had to be discharged and safely landed on the harbour wall at Fishguard.

Discharging the mail and the parcels. Passengers would disembark to one tender whilst their luggage and other goods would be carried by another, to be landed at the Atlantic Wharf. Here, mail bags can be seen sliding down a chute onto the deck of the tender. This card is one of a set of twenty-four produced by the GWR (costing 6d) to promote traffic through the harbour at Fishguard.

The arrival of the *Mauretania*, 1909. The ship was at anchor in the bay, and the passengers are seen here disembarking to the tender Sir Francis Drake. Between 500-600 passengers would often diembark at Fishguard. 'John Cleese', the man in the lower image wearing the boater, is thought to have been a GWR employee since he appears in more than one of this series of postcards.

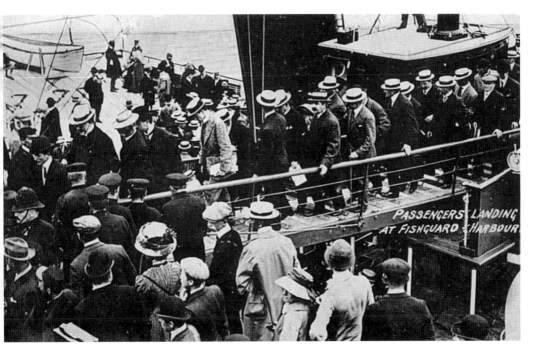

The arrival of the *Mauretania*, 1909. From the big ship to the harbour wall was a distance of a mile or so. Those seeking to save a day by landing at Fishguard were mainly businessmen en route to London or the continent. Following completion of immigration requirements, these passengers, along with mail bags, were whisked away to the train platforms, and thence on one of the 'crack' GWR express trains to Paddington. Baggage vans were attached to the rear of the train.

The arrival of the *Mauretania*, 1909. On the very first visit of the *Mauretania* to Fishguard, a large number of the ladies of Fishguard and Goodwick dressed themselves in Welsh National costume to form a welcoming party for the passengers passing through the port. Here, they are assembled at the harbour prior to the landing of the passengers – posed for a photograph which the GWR were to use in much of their publicity material.

The First *Mauretania* Special to leave Fishguard in 1909 was hauled by two 4-4-0 engines: No. 5402 *Halifax* (City Class) and No. 4108 *Gardenia* of the Flower Class. It was necessary to use two engines to haul the heavy trains up the very steep bank (among the steepest in the United Kingdom, with a gradient of 1 in 50) at Manorowen. A second train, to the left, is also preparing for departure and was hauled by two Flower Class locomotives, No's. 4111 *Anemone* and 4164 *Mignonette*.

The Cunard Liners visit Fishguard: The first Cunard Liner to visit Fishguard was the R.M.S.Mauretania on 30th August 1909. The list shown below is taken from the County Echo for 7th April 1910, and from this, it will be observed that visits would take place of one of the larger liners (Cunard or Booth Line) twice, occasionally three times a week;-

"Appended are the dates and approximate hours of Cunard and Booth Steamers' arrival at Fishguard as officially supplied to us;-

Ship	Date	Time of arrival
Ambrose	April 11th	uncertain
Campania	12th	9.00pm
Mauretania	18th	5.00pm
Caronia	23rd	4.00pm
Augustine	23rd	u/c
Lusitania	25th	6.00pm
Campania	May 2nd	9.00pm
Hilary	2nd	u/c
Carmania	11th	6.30pm
Anselm	13th	u/c
Zealander	15th	
Mauretania	16th	5.00pm
Caronia	21st	4.00pm
Lanfranc	22nd	u/c
Lusitania	23rd	6.00pm
Campania	31st	9.00pm
Carmania	June 4th	6.30pm
Mauretania	6th	
Anthony	12th	u/c
Caronia	18th	4.00pm
Campania	21st	9.00pm
Ambrose	22nd	u/c
Mauretania	27th	4.00pm
Carmania	July 2nd	6.30pm
Hilary	2nd	u/c
Lusitania	4th	5.00pm
Anselm	11th	u/c
Carmania	12th	9.00pm
Caronia	16th	4.00pm
Mauretania	18th	4.00pm

The Cunard ships would call at Fishguard only on their voyages back from the United States, and would remain outside the north breakwater for no more that fifty minutes or so. A typical "discharge" rate shows that on 16th May, a total of 559 passengers disembarked, and a further 1160 mailbags and 2100 items of luggage and packages were off-loaded.

Ocean-going liners visit Fishguard, 1910.

Opposite below: The Cunard Express leaving Fishguard Harbour in 1914. The *Aquitania* paid a brief visit to Fishguard on 16 June 1914, and the photograph shows the Cunard Express of the day just pulling out of Fishguard Harbour. The pair of Flower Class locomotives have been replaced by No. 4040 *Queen Boadicea* of the Star Class, an engine boasting the considerably greater pull of 12½ tons at the draw bar.

Wartime duties for the ships, 1914 – there were none that escaped the war. Ships were commandeered by His Majesty's Government from whatever quarter. Both the *St David* (above) and the *Aquitania* (below) were used as hospital ships. The *Aquitania* was the largest and most sumptuous ship to have visited Fishguard. She cannot have been more than five years old when she was commandeered for wartime service.

seven

Not a Million Miles Away

ST. DOGMAELS, CARDIGAN.

Above: The village of St Dogmaels at the mouth of the Teifi River was the home of the largest shipbuilding yard in South Wales until around 1860. There was a brisk trade from the port of Cardigan (about two miles upstream). The village also had its own Rural District Council, with responsibilities for local administration, and also making provision for the sick and the poor.

Right: Annual Report to the Guardians of the Workhouse, 1914. One of the more sinister aspects of St Dogmaels was the Workhouse. This provided accommodation for 'Indoor Paupers' (IPs), and other assistance for 'Outdoor Paupers' (OPs). In 1914 there were seventy-six IPs. Here is an extract from the Abstract of Accounts for that year.

NEWPORT DISTRICT.   G. Watts Lewis, Relieving Officer.

No.	Name of Pauper.	Age.	Where resident.	Weekly Relief.	Cause of Requiring Relief.	In kind, quantity, and description.	In money.	Remarks.
	Newport :			s. d.			£ s. d.	
1	Ellen Owen	68	King-street	5 0	Idiot		13 1 0	
2	Mary Rees	70	Long-street	5 0	Rheumatism		0 5 0	O.A.P.
3	Eliza Beynon	43	Pen'rallt	4 0	Disease of knee		10 9 0	
4	Alfred Owen	49	King-street	4 0	Blind		10 9 0	
5	Martha John	28	Long-street	4 0	Disease of spine		10 9 0	
6	Mary Rowlands	60	Do.	3/6 4/-	Rheumatism		10 2 0	
7	Mary Evans	63	Parrog	4/- 4/-	Bedridden		13 13 0	Dead
8	Rhoda James	48	Sea View	6 0	Widow & 3 children		15 14 6	Dead
9	Ann Davies	68	King-street	7 0	Bedridden	Burial & Nursing	19 0 0	Discontinued
10	Annie Thomas	43	Factory-lane	3 0	Widow & 2 children		2 5 0	Discontinued
11	David Davies	63	St. Mary-street	5 0	Rheumatism	8yds. shirting flannel	13 10 0	
12	Elizabeth Nicholas	38	Parrog	4 6	Widow & 3 children		2 9 6	
13	Frances John	62	Long-street	1 6	Weakness		3 19 0	
14	Sarah A. Williams	30	Factory-lane	2 6	Heart disease		6 11 0	
15	Thos. Howells	50	Long-street	3/- 4/-	Rheumatism		8 9 0	
16	Maria Williams	66	Ffynonbeder	3/6 4/6	Debility		9 9 0	
17	Ann Prosser	69	King-street	3 0	Old age		7 17 0	
18	Martha Morgan	60	West-street	5 0	Tuberculosis		13 1 0	
19	Rachel Lloyd	45	School House	3 0	Widow & 3 children		7 18 6	
20	Margt. Nicholas	64	St. Mary's-street	4 0	Old age	Con. to Workhouse	9 18 0	Taken to [Workhouse
21	Martha Howells	57	Parrog	4/- 6/6	Paralysed		12 14 0	
22	Maria Evans	54	King-street	3 0	Spinal disease		7 5 0	
23	Hannah Rees	60	Long-street	5 0	Debility		3 19 0	
						Total...£	212 7 6	
	Dinas :							
1	Amos Bowen	43	Bwlchmawr	6 0	Idiot	Con. to Workhouse	7 14 0	Taken to [Workhouse
2	Wm. Thomas	45	Gate	4 0	Cripple	4yds. white & 8 do.	11 2 8	
3	Bella Richards	40	Do.	4 6	Widow & 3 children	[shirting flannel	11 16 6	
4	Bet. Morris	69	Brynhenllan	3/- 3/6 4/-	Debility		9 14 0	
5	Thos. Harries	82	Jericho	5 0	Idiot	1 pr. boots & 2 prs.	13 14 8	
6	Dorothy Morris	63	Cwmyreglwys	5 0	Heart disease	[stockings	13 1 0	
7	Dd. Davies	70	Garnwen	5 0	Rheumatism	3½ yds. drawers	10 4 6	O.A.P.
8	Elizabeth James	48	Cwinyreglwys	3 0	Weakness	[flannel	5 15 6	Discontinued
9	Elizabeth Davies	44	Do.	4 0	Idiot		10 9 0	
10	Lewis Rees	46	Ffynone	4 0	Feeble minded		4 16 0	Removed to [Nevern Par.
11	John Young	53	Clover Hill	12/- 15/-	Blind, wife & 7 ch'ren	Fireguard	37 2 9	[Workhouse
12	Rebecca Jenkins	18	Bwlch-mawr	7 0	Disease of spine		7 15 0	Taken to
13	William Edwards	72	Ffynone		Weakness		0 10 0	O.A.P.
14	Elizabeth Davies	70	Bwlchmawr	3 6	Old age		5 8 6	
						Total...£	149 4 1	
	Eglwyswrw :							
1	Ann Luke	40	Eglwyswrw	2 6	Debility		3 5 0	Discontinued
2	Hannah Thomas	39	Tyddincastell	4 0	Heart disease		3 5 0	
						Total...£	6 10 0	
	Llanfairnantgwyn :							
1	Ann Havard	52	Rhyd-ddu	3 0	Debility		6 19 0	
						Total...£	6 19 0	
	Llanychllwydog :							
	Meline :							
1	Martha James	66	Tynewydd	5 0	Rheumatism		13 8 1	
2	Martha Jenkins	67	Bankyreithin	3/6 4/6	Do.		9 17 10	
3	Thos. Thomas	70	Pantyrodyn	5 0	Weakness		5 15 0	O.A.P.
4	Martha Jones	85	Cwmmins-bach		Bedridden	Nursing	6 10 0	
5	Mary Edwards	61	Cwmsaeson	3 0	Throat complaint	Provisions	1 10 3	
6	Elizabeth Lloyd	57	Penrhyn Castle	5 0	Rheumatism		0 10 0	
						Total...£	37 11 2	
	Nevern :							
1	Jane Jones	60	Pen'rallt-goch	4 0	Idiot		10 9 0	
2	Martha Rees	70	Pwllybroga	4 0	Debility		6 0 0	O.A.P.
3	Elizabeth Llewelyn	44	Berian Cross	7 0	Bedridden	[for son	18 5 0	
4	Louisa Williams	60	Brynberian	4 0	Debility	Outfit & pr. boots	12 7 3	

CORACLE FISHERMEN - CENARTH. 187

Above: The coracle men of Cenarth, *c.* 1900. Coracles have been used on the lower Teifi Valley for centuries, for the netting of salmon, and more recently for the dipping of sheep. In this photograph, they are seen against a background of the bridge at Cenarth, with their nets hanging on the tree beside them.

Left: The Chairman of Eglwyswrw Magistrates was at one time Mrs Gerran Jenkins JP, wife of Mr Islwyn Jenkins who was headmaster at Newport primary school. 'Pedro' (not his real name), a well-known salmon poacher from Newport, was up before the magistrates for illicit removal of fish from the river. Defended by a slick 'silk', the case was dismissed on a technicality. That night, a long brown paper parcel was delivered to Mrs Jenkins' home, Hellespont House, and when it was opened it was found to be a freshly caught salmon – a token of Pedro's appreciation!

The Griffiths family at Trewern, *c.* 1925. Evan James Griffiths was born at a farm called Ysguborwen in 1885. When he was three years old, the family moved to nearby Trewern Farm, which his father farmed until his death in 1910. Two years later, Evan married Mary Jane Howells of Cilgwyn, and the couple had a daughter, Elizabeth Mary (Lit). During a period of convalescence from an illness in her early teens, Sir George Bowen of Llwyngwair brought her a gift of a Persian kitten. The kitten was so beautiful that many lady members of the household wished to be commemorated within the name of this magnificent creature, and the kitten was duly christened Florence Elizabeth Margaret Webb Griffiths. It was only several months later that it was discovered that the animal was a tom cat!

E.J. Griffiths was a farmer who set himself very high standards, and on three occasions won the Champion Beast at the Royal Welsh Show with his Shorthorn bull, Comet. On one occasion, he was unable to use his usual haulage contractor, and used an alternative to carry the bull to the show at Nantgaredig. Shortly before reaching the showground, the animal's legs went through the floor of the lorry, leaving poor Comet to run – *Fred Flintstone* fashion – in the lorry. Nonetheless, Comet stole the show.

The family at Fachongle, *c.* 1900. It has been said on many occasions that 100 years ago, it required no more than three families to fill a chapel. There were thirteen children in this family, and others died during childbirth. From left to right: Maria Jane, who, along with two sisters lived her entire life at Fachongle; David, who fought in the First World War, and then worked in the mining industry, for local roads and maintenance departments, and also farmed a smallholding; Elizabeth who was an accomplished accordion player who entered domestic service at Brithdir Mawr – she was later, sadly, found dead at a house near Bentinck in Newport; Alice, who was one of the three sisters who remained at Fachongle; Margaret, who, after serving elsewhere, entered domestic service at Trewern Farm and who ultimately became a lifelong (sixty years) companion to Mrs Griffiths at Trewern.

Simon (Cwrtbach) (wearing a bowler hat) holding a photograph of John, the only absent child. John spent his life in the Welsh mining industry based at Clydach Vale. The parents Benjamin and Mary Anne (and Rover the dog) sit in front of Simon.

His mother holds George, the youngest member of the family. He undertook work on local farms when he grew up, and lived for many years with his wife Lil at Cilgwyn Mill. Edith (in front), was housekeeper to Morgan and Richardson (Solicitor) at Cae Morgan following which she did the same work at Penwaun, Nevern for Mrs Cobb, the widow of a Royal Naval Commander.

Ann (back row) married James Rees and ran the farm at Pwll following the death of her husband. Martha married a builder called William Morgan who lived in Caerphilly.

Mary was the third of the sisters who remained at Fachongle.

Rose married Dai James of St Dogmaels. He ran a smallholding whilst she conducted the business of the post office at Penfeidr.

Simon was conscripted into the army and undertook military training, but his conscience prevented him from remaining there, He 'escaped' and went into hiding. It is said that the police deliberately failed to find him. He then entered the retail trade ending as manager of the Co-operative stores at Ton y Pandy.

Pleasure flights from Blaenmeini, 1932 The *County Echo* reported on 16 June 1932 that the company Air Travel Ltd. 'gave flights daily over Newport with a magnificent Siddeley-Armstrong aeroplane. The company, who are pioneers of public flying, are making a tour of South Wales under the direction of Captain F.J.V. Holmes and have as their pilots Captain Kingswill, Captain Miller and Captain Kemp'.

As a special treat, Miss Joyce Davies of Llys Meddyg was allowed a trip in the aeroplane over Newport, on the condition that she was accompanied by Mr Bill Lewis of Barclays Bank, Newport. The flight was watched by an enthusiastic gathering from the land at Berry Hill. These included Joyce's parents Mr and Mrs Ernest Davies. However, as the pilot performed a 'loop the loop' over Carningli Mountain, it appears at this juncture that Mrs Davies became so frightened that she fainted!

The beach at Pwllgwaelod, 1905. The community at Pwllgwaelod comprised of little more than can be seen in this photograph, but nonetheless, along with Cwm yr Eglwys, it served as a point of importation of such materials as coal, culm and limestone. The well-known hostelry, The Sailors' Safety can be seen on the right, with the ubiquitous limekilns in the centre, and the port office in between, whilst a ship waits to be lifted by the next tide.

A bill for a 'cargo of lime stones' purchased by William Bennett of Bwlchmawr, Dinas Cross. He was an 'entrepreneur extraordinaire', and receipts recently discovered at his house indicate that he was a grocer, baker, draper, milliner, builders' merchant, agricultural merchant, brewer and publican, ironmonger and chemist. He was an ardent churchgoer, and contributed substantially, financially and otherwise, towards the development of education in the community.

Strumble Head lighthouse, *c.* 1910. The need for a lighthouse at Strumble Head had been recognised, and it was proposed in Trinity House records as early as 1825. This replaced a lightship situated in the south of Cardigan Bay, and a beacon arrangement situated on the coast near this point. The facility was built in 1908-'09 on the island of Ynys Meicel. Powered by paraffin, it was converted to electricity in 1949, and fitted with a Tannoy fog signal in 1969. Around 1980, the lighthouse became fully automated, and was controlled from St Ann's lighthouse near Dale.

Although the Radio Station above the harbour at Fishguard was completed by August 1912, it was not formally opened until 8 September 1913. Only six radio stations had been established in the United Kingdom at this time, and the two nearest to Fishguard were in Cornwall and Rosslare. After much persuasion, the Posts and Telegraphs authorities acceded to the GWR request that the station at Rosslare should be transferred to Fishguard, on condition that the comapny provided the land, the mast and an electrical power supply to the facility. The mast was transported from Seaforth in England, and was fifty feet high.

The ketch *Crescent* at Porthgain awaits the tide before venturing towards the quay wall where the two young men gaze out to sea. She was built at Cowes in 1887, registered at Aberystwyth, and her master was John Russan of Milford Haven. She was typical of the small sailing vessels involved in the coastal trade around Britain.

The Port of Porthgain, 1930. The port was extremely busy during the first quarter of the twentieth century. Granite was extracted here from two quarries called Caersalem and Jerusalem. A train of wagons can be seen on the skyline tipping rock into the crushers. Bricks were also manufactured here. Slates were cut at Abereiddy, a small inlet $1\frac{1}{2}$ miles to the west, and brought by rail to Porthgain for export. It was not unusual to see as many as six steamers crammed into this tiny harbour.

The stagecoach for Fishguard and Rosebush station, c. 1878. In order to 'export' his slate from Rosebush quarries to his markets in Bristol and elsewhere, Edward Cropper secured authority from the Board of Trade in 1872 to build $8\frac{1}{2}$ miles of railway from Rosebush to Narberth Road (Clynderwen), thus linking up with the Great Western Railway. It also provided an opportunity for passengers to travel by rail to Rosebush and thence by coach to Fishguard. The passenger rail link was established in 1876 although its existence as a passenger carrying line did not last long. The horse-drawn coach provided accommodation for First, Second and Third class passengers. First class passengers could sit inside, protected from the weather, whilst the Second class passengers could enjoy a seat outside, but were, nonetheless, exposed to the weather. The Third class passengers just had to hang on to the coach wherever they could! The ten-mile journey to Fishguard was an easy one, except for the steep 1 in 4 gradient at Trebover Hill between Llanychaer and Fishguard. Here it is said that First class passengers could remain in their seats Second class passengers had to dismount and walk up the hill whilst the Third class passengers had to get off and push!

Opposite below: The North Pembrokeshire Railway at Rosebush, c. 1932. A controlling interest in the line was acquired by a Birmingham solicitor, Joseph Rowlands, in 1892. After Rowlands had threatened to sell to the London and North West Railway (LNWR), the GWR reluctantly agreed to purchase the line in 1898. Passenger services were provided until October 1937 and for the carriage of goods until May 1949.

Workers' cottages at Rosebush, *c.* 1930. The volume of business transacted in the Rosebush quarries grew to such an extent that it was necessary to build further housing for the workforce. Terraces totalling twenty-six cottages were built comprising of one room upstairs and another down, with a further lean-to kitchen added later. These were let to the workers for £2 per annum, and were very much sought after.

The Dressing Shed at Rosebush quarry, 1930. Also known as Rosebush Mill, this building was used for the shaping, dressing and cutting the slates to size It had a great advantage in that the slates could be directly loaded on to standard gauge wagons obviating the need for labour intensive handling at a later stage. At one time, the quarries, with an output of more than 5,000 tons per annum, employed more than a 100 men.

Acknowledgements

I would like to offer my sincere thanks to the following for supplying me with photographs or facts, and my equally sincere thanks and apologies to those whom I may have inadvertently omitted: Edwina Adams, Pamela Baldwin, Mair Childs, Doris Davies, Enid Davies, the late Jack Davies, Mefyn and Iwan Davies, Dewi Evans, Penry Evans, Eira Griffiths, Jean Griffiths, Gwyneth and Alan Hayward, Jenny Howells, John Hughes, Lily James, Phyllis John, the late May Jones and Joyce Joy, David and Joan Lewis, William Lewis, Martin Mathias, the late Vera Morgan and Hazel Owen, Ieuan Owen, John Evans and the Pembrokshire Coast National Park, the late William Scarr, Nick Thomas, Chris Taylor, Ryan Thomas, Bertie Vaughan, Eric Williams, Ken Williams, Jimmy Williams and Valmai Williams.

Mrs Vera Phillips and Mrs Ann Lewis-Smith have been particularly generous in allowing me to use their Newport Women's Institute scrap book, but unfortunately, it has not been possible to use as many photographs and images as one had hoped. The ladies of the Carningli Women's Institute have gifted me with many local history books for my collection from which much of the information presented has been gleaned. Happily, both WIs were reunited on 11 February 2003.

The author would also like to thank Miss Fran Gannon and Miss Katherine Burton of the Tempus Publishing Company for their friendly assistance, and also for their patience and forbearing in dealing with those difficulties which inevitably arise when one attempts to solve problems 'at a distance'.

Apart from my mother, Mrs Lit Lewis, who, in her ninetieth year remains a constant source of information and inspiration, I would like to tender my warmest thanks to Alderman Dillwyn Miles for scrutinising and checking the accuracy of the script, and his assistance and constructive comment at all times. Finally, my sincere thanks go to Dr Geraint Jenkins for writing a much-appreciated foreword for this book.